Mildred B. Foss teaches machine embroidery
at Renton Vocational-Technical Institute, Renton Washington.
She is the author of *Zigzag Variables, Unlimited* and
of several articles for *Popular Handicraft Hobbies Magazine*.

MILDRED B. FOSS

Creative Embroidery with Your Sewing Machine

A SPECTRUM BOOK

PRENTICE-HALL, INC., ENGLEWOOD CLIFFS, NEW JERSEY

Library of Congress Cataloging in Publication Data

Foss, Mildred B
    Creative embroidery with your sewing machine.

    (The Creative handcrafts series)   (A Spectrum Book)
    Includes index.
    1. Embroidery, Machine. I. Title.
TT772.F67   746.4'4   76-7588
ISBN 0-13-189365-3
ISBN 0-13-189357-2 pbk.

Printed in the United States of America

Prentice-Hall International, Inc., *London*
Prentice-Hall of Australia Pty. Limited, *Sydney*
Prentice-Hall of Canada, Ltd., *Toronto*
Prentice-Hall of India Private Limited, *New Delhi*
Prentice-Hall of Japan, Inc., *Tokyo*
Prentice-Hall of Southeast Asia Pte. Ltd., *Singapore*

Contents

v

Preface

"Do I have to be an experienced sewer in order to get into your machine embroidery classes?" This is the question many students ask me before they sign up for classes I teach at Renton Vocational-Technical Institute at Renton, Washington.

I have been sewing for less than five years. My husband bought me a super-automatic sewing machine for our silver wedding anniversary, and the only thing I had ever sewn before were some drapes (with the aid of a drapery instruction book), on my old straight-stitch machine. Occasionally I did reinforce a rip here and there as our six children were growing up. That was the extent of my sewing expertise.

The firm that sold him the sewing machine made it clear that I should come in for lessons so I could become fully acquainted with the machine, but I never was able to go. So I experimented on my own, and soon found out just how much versatility a zig-zag sewing machine has. In no time, through trial and error and tangled threads, I was writing words and "painting" little scenes with my machine. Because I had not had much artistic experience before, this new art form really fascinated me.

After that, I contacted sewing machine stores, libraries, and bookstores, always searching for books on machine embroidery. When I couldn't find one, I decided there would have to be one.

This book contains step-by-step instructions on how to set the sewing machine properly for various techniques, and the embroidery techniques are explained simply and clearly. You can make several kinds of wall plaques, "jean scenes," unusual gifts, monogrammed towels and linens, unique designs on clothing and costumes, and dozens of other articles and garments by following the instructions in this book.

You can feel confident as you try the different setups, for all the difficulties I encountered have already been untangled. If you follow the instructions chapter by chapter, you won't have any of the trouble I went through, for the instructions can be understood by anyone with little or no previous experience with sewing. So dust off your sewing machine and get out your scrap bag and half-used spools of thread. You're going to learn to do creative embroidery—with your sewing machine.

Acknowledgments

Sincere thanks to the following for their valuable assistance in the preparation of this book:

Husqvarna Viking Company, for providing the illustrations for Figures 1.1(g–j), 1.19(a), 4.4, 4.20, 4.24, and 5.16.

Mr. and Mrs. Chuck Diggs of Viking Sewing Machine Center, Renton, Washington, for supplying me with the latest Viking Sewing Machine.

The Singer Sewing Machine Company for Singer Touch and Sew Model 600E, which contained the superchain stitch; Elesa McBride of Auburn, Washington, for demonstrating it.

Mr. and Mrs. Dick Smith of Kent Vacuum and Sewing Center, for the loan of an Elna Sewing Machine for hemstitching.

Mrs. Jack (Muriel) Thompson of Kent, Washington, for her beautiful embroidered bouquet wall plaque, table dressing, and brushed-denim shirt.

Mrs. Dean (Dorothy) Ringer, sewing teacher at Renton

Vocational-Technical Institute, Renton, Washington, for her pillow with fringe.

Mr. Curt Ojala (BEST PHOTOS, 3041 S. 274th Street, Auburn, Washington), who was responsible for the photography.

All sewing was done by the author, with the exception of the articles provided by Mrs. Thompson and Mrs. Ringer.

What You Can Do with Your Sewing Machine

1

In this chapter we will discuss the various parts of your sewing machine and some of the basic stitches you will be using when you begin to embroider with your machine. You will get acquainted with some of your special machine attachments, as well as a few "extras" that will become an important part of your useful and exciting new hobby. And you'll find out how to make some creative things right away! So get ready for your first adventure in embroidery with your sewing machine.

KNOW YOUR MACHINE

Machine embroidery is so unlimited that there is no end to the many ways you can enhance your wardrobe as well as your home. Today you see embroidery on shoes, purses, jeans, lingerie, on yokes and sleeves of blouses, and on placemats, table napkins, and tablecloths. In addition, there are many different

kinds of embroidered wall plaques and chair covers, not to men-
tion the lovely machine embroidery used to embellish such
things as the very chic ultrasuede shirt-dresses and coats.

The embroiderer will wonder: how can stitches such as the
cross stitch, long and short stitch, French knot, padded satin
stitch, and so on possibly be done on a machine? These fancy
stitches *can* be done, as surely as you can sew a plain seam, but
the first requisite is to fully acquaint yourself with your zigzag-
type sewing machine. True, many things can be done using the
straight-stitch machine or even a treadle model. But in this
modern age, and with the availability of fabulous fabrics and
sewing notions, a zigzag machine should be standard equip-
ment in the home of anyone interested in creative needlework, much on a par with the kitchen range. If you can turn out
a meal cooked at the proper temperature merely by setting the
proper dials, why not learn to set the dials of the sewing machine and turn out embroidery that looks good enough to eat?

Study the manual that came with your machine, and if it requires oiling, clean and oil it regularly according to the instructions. If you have a machine that does not require oiling, so
much the better, but brush it periodically. If you own the free-

Fig. 1.1 (a) Various parts of the sewing machine; (b) feed dog
(goes up and down); (c) extension plate; (d) throat plate or needle
plate; (e) ankle; (f) foot; (g) slot needle; (h) wing needle;
(i) embroidery hoops; (j) cutting needle for leather.

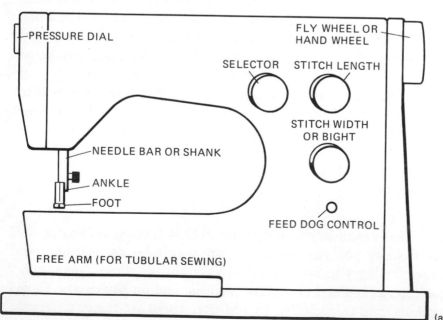

PRESSURE DIAL

FLY WHEEL OR
HAND WHEEL

SELECTOR   STITCH LENGTH

STITCH WIDTH
OR BIGHT

NEEDLE BAR OR SHANK

ANKLE

FOOT

FEED DOG CONTROL

FREE ARM (FOR TUBULAR SEWING)

(a)

arm model, attach the extension plate, for a flat surface is mandatory in machine embroidery. Be sure you arrange a space in which the lighting is good and you have lots of elbow room. And don't forget to plug in your machine!

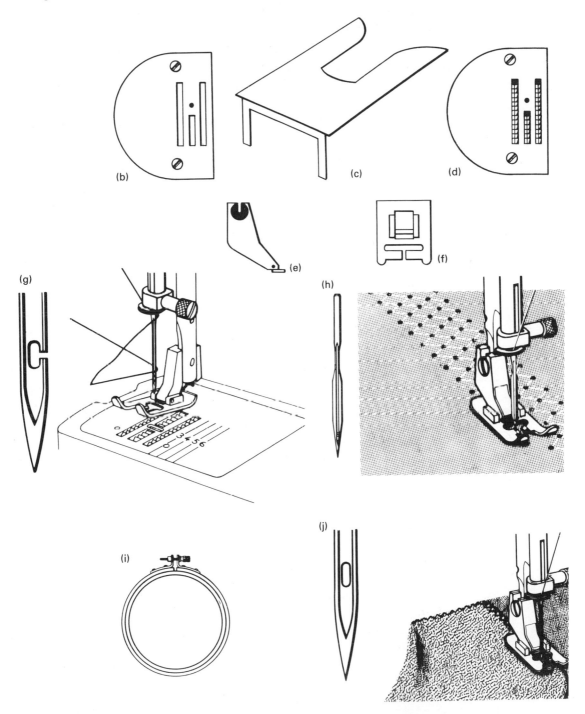

To get acquainted with your machine, thread up with one color in the spool and a different color in the bobbin. You will find that having two colors will help you learn to adjust the tension. Use any thread you have on hand, but refer to the manual for the size needle to use with that particular size thread. If you use polyester thread, be sure to thread it through the machine and needle in the same direction as it comes from the spool. This will prevent any scruffing at the needle. The needle should be sharp; if you have any difficulty threading a machine needle, buy slot needles—they don't require threading. You pass the thread along the needle until the thread glides into the slot.

Have you seen a pincushion that resembles a tomato with a much smaller tomato attached to it by a cord? The smaller tomato is an emery bag, and if you push the needle in and out of it several times, it will clean and sharpen well. Do not store any needles in the emery bag, however—use the larger pincushion for that purpose.

There is also another way to keep needles sharp. A 6″ × 2″ rectangle called a "needle-sharpening pad" can be found at the sewing notions counter. To use this, simply unthread your sewing machine needle, put the stitch length at longest, and run the bare needle back and forth over the pad.

While we are on the subject of notions, you must have an accessories box for the usual trinkets you'll need for sewing. Do you have your basic supplies? Here is a list of supplies you will need for the basics of machine embroidery. Later we will discuss other things you will need.

Two colors of thread (machine embroidery thread if you have some; however, any thread will do)
One set of 8″ wooden hoops, with a screw on larger hoop
Heavy grade of muslin or scrap felt
Embroidery scissors or snippers
Dressmaker's carbon paper
Sharp sewing machine needles
Soft pencil (# 2)
Transfer pencil
4   Tracing paper

Let's begin by using a 12″ square piece of practice material. Set the machine stitch length on *longest*. Check the tension. Tensions run from 0 to 10, usually, with 5 being about normal. Set the tension on normal, pressure on normal, and refer to your own manual again if necessary. The pressure controls the presser foot; sometimes you need a heavy foot, sometimes lighter. Check your zigzag control to make sure it is on 0 or off. These settings are usually taught to you when you purchase the machine. They are included here for those who might be using a classroom machine, or have purchased one second-hand and therefore did not receive the lessons on how to operate the machine. Attach the *regular* presser foot.

THE REGULAR SETUP

The Straight Stitch and Backstitch

Now, sew a row of straight stitching approximately 4 inches long. Clip the threads from both the beginning and the end. Move to the right of your row and begin another row; but this time push the reverse button and stitch backward for a stitch or two (If your machine does not have a reverse button, again refer to your manual to find out how to make your machine sew backward.) Now, both at the beginning and at the end of the line of stitching, add two or three stitches in reverse to lock in the threads.

The setup you have just used is known as the *regular setup*; the stitches you have just learned are the *straight stitch* and the *backstitch*.

Look at your two rows and check for proper tension by examining the thread. Does the bobbin thread show through to the top stitching? If so, *loosen* the tension just a bit and try again, but do not change anything about the bobbin. This is the reason for using a different color in the bobbin—it will make it easier for you to learn how to obtain the correct tension.

5

Now put the tension on 2 points below normal. If your normal is 5, set the tension on 3. Put the stitch length on 3 and sew a wavy line, backstitching at both the beginning and end. Clip the threads and then sew a large U, using the same technique. With the looser tension you are no longer confined to straight lines of sewing, but instead are free to move the material and follow lines of curves and dips.

The setup you have just used is known as the *automatic set-up*. See how easy it is?

MAKING AND USING A PATTERN

Now let's apply what we have learned so far by tracing the design in Figure 1.2. Place a sheet of tracing paper over the design. Because this particular design has no lettering in it, it doesn't make any difference which way you use it, so take the shortcut and trace the design by using the transfer pencil. Go over the whole design just as though you were using an ordinary lead pencil, then turn the paper over and place the transfer lines against the fabric you plan to use for your potholder. A

Fig. 1.2 Potholder pattern.

6

heavier fabric is easy to use in this case, because you will be working without hoops, and will be continually turning the material around.

Pin the pattern to the material, and with the iron set for fairly hot, rest the iron on the paper for a few seconds—not ironing, merely pressing. In a matter of seconds the design will be transferred to the material. If it doesn't show plainly, just add a touch with the lead pencil. Always make sure your transfer pencil is very sharp, because if it isn't, your lines will come out too wide, and it takes many washings to get them out—sometimes they will never come out.

There is an easy way to make sure the lines are *very* thin; this is to use transfer ink. However, when ink is used, the motif traced onto the tissue paper must dry for several hours or overnight before it is transferred to the material; and this is bothersome. The advantage in using ink is that the pattern washes out during the very first wash. Transfer ink is made by using equal parts of sugar and blueing, and is applied with a stylus or a dried-up ballpoint pen.

Linear Stitching and Pivoting

With the machine setup on *automatic*, stitch over the lines of the design, making sure your thread color contrasts well with the material. Use any stitch length you prefer, but you will get better results if you use longer stitches on the straight lines and tiny, short ones on curves. Remember to backstitch at the beginning and end—wherever you must clip the thread to start another line of stitching. Periodically you might have to raise the presser bar in order to turn the material around. When you do this, be sure to keep the needle *in* the material. This is called *pivoting*. If you feel that the machine goes too fast for you and you keep getting off the lines, let up more of the pedal. Of course if your machine has a reduction gear, employ that, and it will slow the stitching down. The reduction gear is either a button or a knob found on most zigzag sewing machine models and is usually marked with the words "slow, fast" or "low, high." Set it on low or slow.

Once the stitching is complete, raise the presser bar and remove the material from the machine. Clip all threads from both the front and back sides of the material. This is simply good housekeeping. Take a look at the completed work. We call this *linear* stitching. See Figure 1.3.

Fig. 1.3   Potholder design done in linear stitch.

The Automatic Satin Stitch

There are times when linear stitching doesn't stand out too well. In these cases, set the stitch-*width* button on #2. This button or knob is also known as the zigzag knob; it gives width to the straight stitch and linear stitching. The width can vary from 0 to 7, but the average zigzag machine goes no wider than #4. Change the stitch *length* to very short or 3. (Caution: the stitch-*length* knob is different from the stitch-*width* knob, it is graduated from 0 to 4 but also has a micro-graduation between 0 and 0.5, permitting precision adjustment of the smaller stitch lengths.) With this setup go over the whole design again, backstitching as before. If you did not use a heavier material before, you may find it difficult to swing your material around, and the stitches may pile up. It is a waste of time to remove any poor stitching, so correct the situation by placing a scrap piece of **8**   typing paper or even a scrap fabric under the material. Of course, the fabric will be there to stay, whereas the paper will tear away. Does the added width produce a more pronounced design rather than a delicate-appearing stitch? Widen the stitch width to #4 and fill in the left eye of the design. You have now completed the *automatic satin stitch.*

Quilting

POTHOLDERS. Take any of your thicker scrap pieces—such as from an old quilted robe or an old towel—from the rag bag and cut a piece large enough to come within ¼" of the edge of the piece you just completed in automatic satin stitch. Make sure it is thick enough material for a potholder. Now cut another piece of material like the one on which you did the automatic satin stitch—this will serve as the back side of your potholder. Pin all three layers together with safety pins, sandwiching the thick layer in the middle.

The setup should now be changed to *regular* and with the longest stitch. Starting at one corner, sew diagonally across to the opposite corner, remembering to backstitch.

Does your machine have a hole through the shank? Refer to Figure 1.1. Do you have an edge guide (see Fig. 1.4) in your

Fig. 1.4 Edge guide showing quilting.

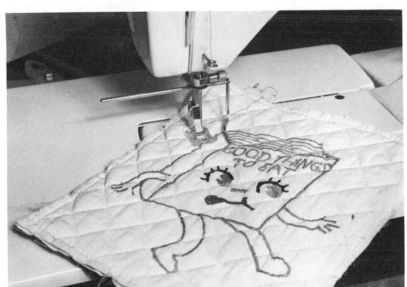

accessories box? Put the guide through the shank, turning the screw to hold the guide intact. Place the potholder under the needle about ¾" to the left of the diagonal line of stitching you just did. Tighten the edge guide over the stitching. Keeping your eye on the edge guide, sew across the potholder. Repeat until the whole side is completed, then turn the potholder around and do the same with the other side. Turn the potholder again and do the same thing you just completed, except that now you cross the lines, making diamond shapes as you sew. You now have completed *machine quilting*.

If you want your next potholder to be stiffer, place the edge guide not more than ½" from the diagonal row; if you want more flexibility, make the rows farther apart. By keeping your eye always on the guide rather than on the needle, you cannot help but get uniformity in your quilting. Finish the potholder by sewing some bias tape around the outside edges, leaving an inch or so of tape for a loop for hanging.

See all the things you can do with your zigzag machine al-

Fig. 1.5　Finished potholder.

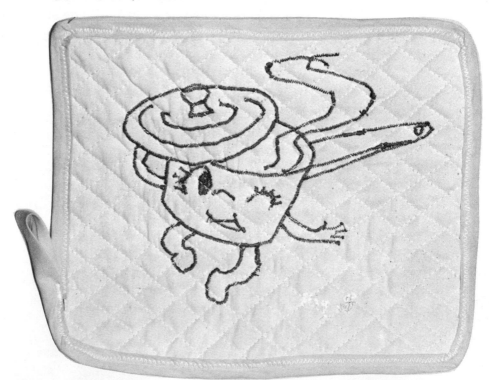

ready, and in only one lesson? Why not go to the fabric store and invest in a package of hot-iron transfers in the "animated kitchen" category, then make different designs on several other potholders with dishtowels to match. This will give you invaluable practice.

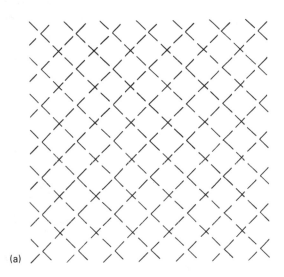

(a)

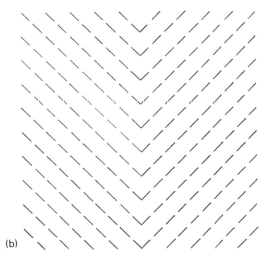

(b)

Fig. 1.6(a, b)   Quilting patterns.

The patterns shown in Figure 1.6 are more suited to machine quilting, because they are set on the diagonal or bias. It might be necessary to adjust the pressure, so check your manual under "presser adjustments" and adjust the pressure as necessary.

WALL PLAQUES IN 3-D.   While linear and satin stitching is fresh in your mind from making the potholder design, how would you like to make a large wall plaque for your home? Look in the fabric stores for pieces of fabric suitable for the room in which you wish to hang the plaque. Figure 1.7 shows some examples of fabric found in the drapery or upholstery sections or in the regular yardage department.

Fig. 1.7   Novelty materials.

Once you have the piece of material you want, find a piece of scrap material for backing. (Usually a sheet or pillow case is good.) Place the two materials flat on the table. Pin them together with straight pins just long enough to hold the backing in place temporarily. Using the automatic setup, do a linear stitch around the main sections of each part of the motif. Notice that the completed wall plaques in Figure 1.8 are done in zigzag stitch in order to call your attention to the various parts of the design of the fabric. Do yours in linear stitch; however, we will talk about zigzag stitching later in the chapter. A stitch length of 3 would work well for this. Start in the center of the design and do the main parts first.

Fig. 1.8 Two 3-D wall plaques.

Once the stitching is complete, turn the piece over and make small slits in each portion of the design between the stitching lines. Stuff either polyester fiberfill or pieces of old nylon hosiery into each portion, packing firmly. Sew up the small slits or staple them together, and the material is ready for framing.

To prepare your piece for framing, place the finished material on a piece of plywood or other strong backing, cut just a bit smaller than the material. Pulling the material very taut, tack or staple the piece to the board, allowing absolutely no wrinkles. This will push against the stuffing, causing the 3-D effect. It is now ready for the frame. You can custom frame it or buy a frame from the hardware or craft store. Frames come packaged in all sizes, and you can finish it in any color or stain you think would look best with your walls and room.

You have just completed a three-dimensional wall plaque. Wasn't it easy?

The Zigzag Stitch

Those of you who own a treadle or straight-stitch machine can certainly make the wall plaque, but you cannot do any satin stitching. There is, however, an attachment on the market called a "zigzag attachment" or "zigzagger" which sells for less than $5. With this attachment, you can zigzag on your machine too.

Let's practice a little zigzagging. Whether you have the built-

Fig. 1.9   Zigzag attachment.

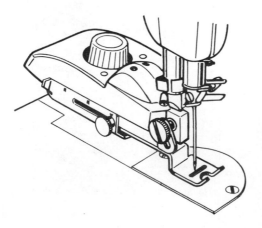

in zigzag or the zigzag attachment, set the machine for the *regular* setup with the stitch length on 2. Now turn your stitch-*width* knob (as shown in Fig. 1.1) and set it on #2. Proceed to stitch a row, backstitching at both ends. Move over to the right of the row you just made and put the presser foot down, but raise the needle. With the needle up, change the width to #4 and make another row of zigzag stitches. Do not fail to raise the needle whenever you change the stitch width. Make another row, leaving the stitch width on #4 but changing the stitch *length* to 4. By changing the stitch length to 4, you changed the zigzag stitch into a satin stitch. From now on, the stitch width will be known as the *bight.*

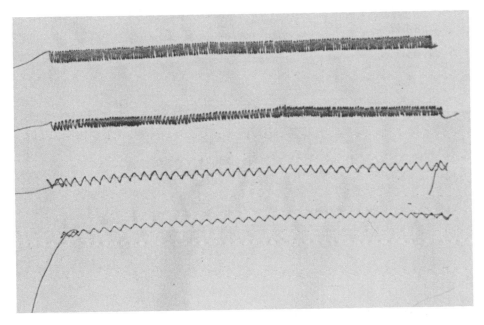

Fig. 1.10   Zigzag and satin stitch.

Scallops

Because scallops are so popular, it is very important to learn them. They can be made in any size you want; you can use a cup, saucer, or plate for larger patterns. Even the embroidery hoops can serve as a pattern for scallops or circles. For now, a plastic ruler with different sizes will make a perfect pattern.

Trace the scallops from Figure 1.11 just as you traced before. Use at least a medium-weight material and a contrasting

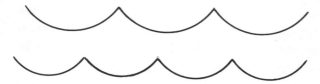

Fig. 1.11   Scallop pattern.

thread color. If you have a *pattern* foot, use it; it has a raised groove on its underside which allows for raised satin stitch and other kinds of stitches. If you don't have one, but plan on buying one, buy the transparent foot—it will let you watch your work better.

Fig. 1.12   Scallops on a dress.

16

Use the *automatic* setup, a stitch length of 4, and a wide bight—#4 or #5. Set the needle into the beginning line of the scallop pattern, with the needle in its *left* position. Follow along the pattern line until you come to the bottom of the first scallop. Push the material under the presser foot just a bit and sew to the very tip of the scallop. Leaving the needle in on the *left*, raise the presser bar, pivot the *material* to the left, then lower the presser bar—the next few satin stitches should fall into place over the last few just done. Repeat this technique until all the scallops are finished.

The 1½″ scallop is often used on hems of decorated dresses as well as around the décolleté (low neckline). The scallops shown in Figure 1.12 were traced on just ½″ from the edges, decorated, and the excess edge was then cut away.

CAMS

Cams are little disks that can be inserted into the super-automatic machines for a number of special stitches. Most machines have several built-in cams, with allowances made for dropping in additional cams. These disks have an automatic

Fig. 1.13 Five rows of cam stitches.

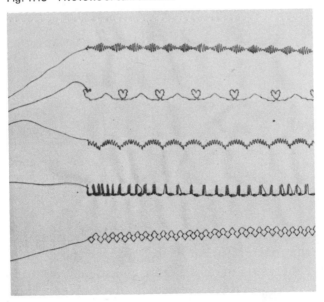

reversing movement to them to allow you to produce more intricate designs automatically.

To use a cam, set your machine up for *automatic*, use the pattern foot, and thread up with a color that contrasts with your material. Drop in a cam and make a row. Change cams and make another row. Try out several of your cam designs.

Symmetrical Stitches

In making multiple rows of automatic cam designs, care must be taken to match up the rows perfectly. If you wish to sew a symmetrical border, always begin in the middle. Sew the next row to either side of the middle row. Study Figure 1.14, which shows seven rows of cam stitches. Using one cam for the center, make the first row. Then change cams and make a row to the right of center. Using that same cam, make a row to the left of the center row. Change cams and make rows four and five; change cams again and make rows six and seven.

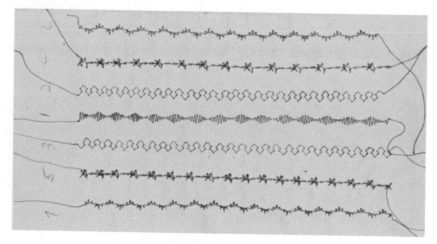

Fig. 1.14   Seven rows of symmetrical cam stitches.

Asymmetrical Stitches

If the pattern stitch itself is asymmetrical, you will have to turn the material when you sew the opposite side. You will be sewing one side of center from top to bottom and the other side from bottom to top, as shown in Figure 1.15.

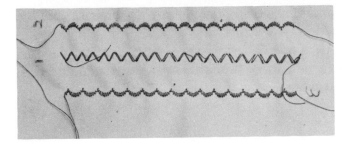
Fig. 1.15 Asymmetrical cam stitches (three rows).

As the end of a row is reached, you should note just where in the cam you are, because you don't necessarily end at the same part of the cam that you wish to start with at the top of the new row. Remove the garment material and substitute a scrap. Sew along on the scrap until you reach the *exact* position of the cam at which you must begin the next row. Slip out the scrap and put the garment back under the needle and make the row. This procedure makes for perfect alignment.

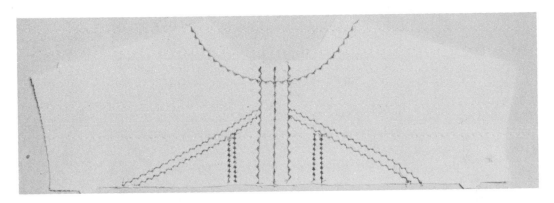
Fig. 1.16 Yoke showing perfect alignment of cam stitches.

Fig. 1.17
Double- and triple-needle stitching.

DOUBLE AND TRIPLE NEEDLES

You can further the versatility of a cam by using two or even three needles and different colors. Keep the bight at no wider than 1½ when using three and no more than 2½ when using two needles, because the added needles have taken up the room allowed for zigzagging except for a small leeway.

19

So many different embroidery stitches can be made simply by combining many different cams and/or combining many different colors. There is no end to the dozens of beautiful decorations you can turn out. Just a few from more than hundreds of designs are shown here.

Fig. 1.18   Combinations of cam stitching.

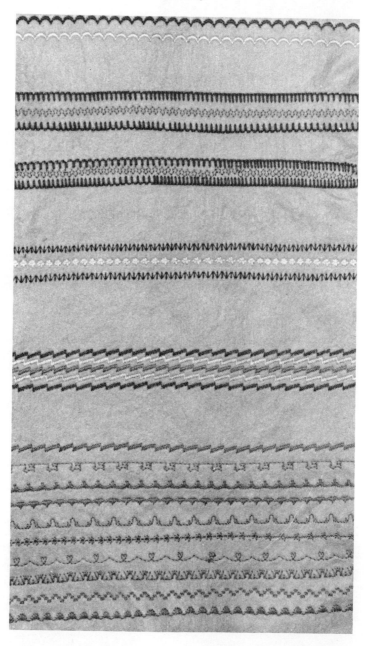

The Shell Stitch

For those of you who have no cams but have a zigzag attachment or a built-in zigzag, you can make an attractive *shell stitch*. This is often used on nylon tricot slips and nighties. Select your blindstitch setting (the one used for hemming clothing without showing any stitches on the right side of the hem), set the stitch length and the bight on 2½, and increase the tension to 7. Finger-press the edge of your garment under slightly and sew along. A beautiful shell stitch is then made automatically.

Fig. 1.19(a, b)   Shell stitch.

(a)

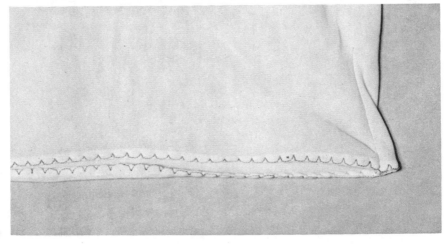

(b)

Lettuce Edging

The popular *lettuce edging* seen in scarves and lingerie can be done by using a tiny zigzag. Cancel out the blindstitch and use a 1½-stitch length and bight. Pull your material taut both from front and back while you sew along the raw edge. The more elasticity to the material, the better. The lettuce edge gives the appearance of cording. This is the quickest way to hem the raw edges of sheer nylon tricot.

Fig. 1.20   Lettuce stitch.

Curves and Circles

So far we have done only straight lines with cams. With the setup on automatic, we can turn the straight lines into curves just as we did earlier. However, we can go a step further into cam designs. There is on the market an attachment known as the "flower stitcher." This attachment works well on any zigzag machine with cams, as long as the *feed dogs* can be pushed away—for the attachment has its own *feed dogs*. (The feed dogs are the teeth that go up and down directly under your needle, to push the material along.) Turn to any cam you wish and this attachment will automatically turn the straight lines into perfect circles of various sizes.

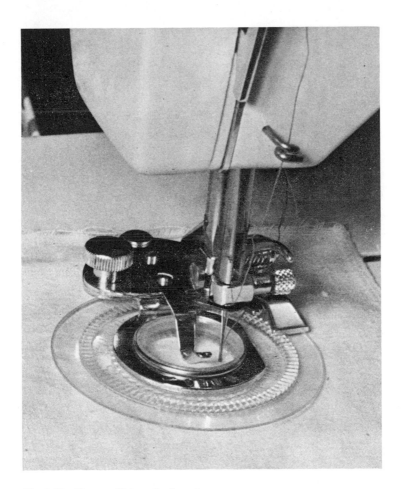

Fig. 1.21 Flower-stitcher attachment.

Look again at the automatic cam designs shown in Figure 1.13. With the "flower stitcher" the designs shown in that illustration are shown in sequential order in Figure 1.22.

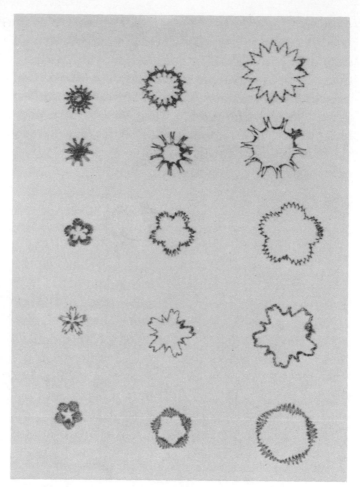

Fig. 1.22   Five rows of circles from flower stitcher.

As you made the circles, did you notice that when you merely stepped on the pedal, the attachment did everything for you? If you forgot to let up on the pedal, it merely went around again until you lifted your foot. Notice also, the *material* goes around as well. This could be rather cumbersome on a large garment, so when you want to decorate, say, the yoke of a shirt, do it *before* you sew the yoke into the garment. The yoke alone turns easily, and with the flower stitcher, it is unnecessary to use hoops. (We will talk about these later.) With certain cams, the circles turn out looking like flowers; other cams make designs more like snowflakes. You are free to add a stem or some other bit on your own, by adding a satin stitch.

Often, when you use the automatic setup, it becomes necessary to keep the material more taut than can be done with the hands. When this is the case, we use embroidery hoops. The hoops should be 8″ in diameter and the larger hoop should have a screw. How can we get the hoops to go under the pattern foot or regular foot we have been using?

Take the empty hoops and try to place them under the foot. Usually, there just isn't that much *give* to the presser foot, and since you must use your foot and the hoops simultaneously, it just isn't practical to keep removing the foot and ankle each time the hoops must go under. If your machine has a vibrator dial or a button marked "darning" or perhaps it is called "presser foot pressure dial," merely use it to turn the pressure completely off. Test it by raising and lowering the presser bar. If there is no resistance, you are all set to place your hoops under the pattern foot. Reset the pressure, however, before beginning to sew. Then, when you want to remove the hoops, once again engage the pressure button. Practice engaging and disengaging the knob until you can insert the hoops easily.

Fig. 1.23   Loaded hoops under needle.

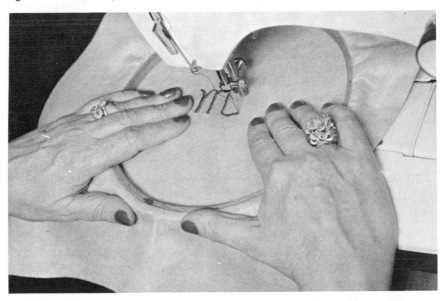

Now take a piece of material about 12 inches square. Separate the hoops and place the material over the larger ring. Loosen the screw on the larger ring and insert the smaller ring over the material and into the larger ring, pulling the material taut and then tightening the screw. Insert the hoops under the foot just as you did when you practiced with the empty hoop. The material rests against the flat bed of the sewing machine, just opposite to the position used in hand embroidery. Unless you place the hoops this way, the needle will never "take."

The Cross Stitch

Trace a few larger cross stitches on your material, set up for *automatic* and use a #2 bight. Load the hoops and place them under the needle.

Fig. 1.24   Cross-stitch pattern.

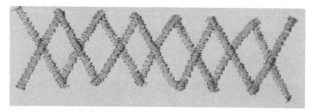

Fig. 1.25   Cross-stitch embroidery.

Position the needle to the right of the cross-stitch line, then backstitch. Do a satin stitch on down to the bottom of the first line; then, leaving the needle in the *left* position, pivot, and proceed up the next line. Repeat until all the "W"-looking lines are done; then backstitch and clip the threads. Turn the material around until you again have a line of "W"-looking lines to fill, and once again follow the same procedure—pivoting *left* on all bottom lines, and pivoting *right* on all upper lines.

Remove the hoops from the machine, and while the material is still intact in the hoops, clip the thread ends from both the front and back.

Gingham Squares Cross Stitching

There are other methods of cross stitching that may be more to your liking; one is to use gingham squares. Because gingham is available with squares of several sizes, all you have to do is pick out a cross-stitch pattern and buy the size gingham you like. In the cross-stitch pattern envelope, there is usually a chart that serves as a guide for any size gingham squares. All you do is follow the squares on the paper with the squares of the gingham, marking the squares with a pencil. (This is not the same as transferring a pattern.)

In the case of tiny cross stitches, you will have to merely cover the crosses with a tiny satin stitch using a #1 bight or less. Begin at the left side and go across, doing all the tiny W's. Then, without turning the hoops at all, work your way back over all the tiny M's.

Fig. 1.26 Gingham squares.

In using hoops, if it becomes necessary to move the material over, instead of removing the material, hoops, and all from under the needle, merely loosen the screw on the larger ring, pull the material over to where you want it, insert the smaller ring, and tighten the screw.

By now you are sufficiently acquainted with machine embroidery to go into free-motion embroidery, for which there is relatively little or no tradition.

2 Free-Motion Embroidery

Now that you have learned some of the basic machine embroidery stitches, you are ready to really unleash your creative urges—with the free-motion technique. For this we begin a new chapter, because free-motion embroidery is really the next big step in your emergence as a sewing machine artist.

THE FREE-MOTION SETUP

Free-motion embroidery is so named because it enables us to do almost any design we want to. You might say we take the machine out of gear and put it into neutral in order to sew as free as a bird. To start, we turn the tension to zero, push away the feed dogs (this automatically cancels out the stitch length), and all we use is the presser bar and the bight. We bare the needle, for we use no ankle, no foot, no cams—just a bare needle and thread.

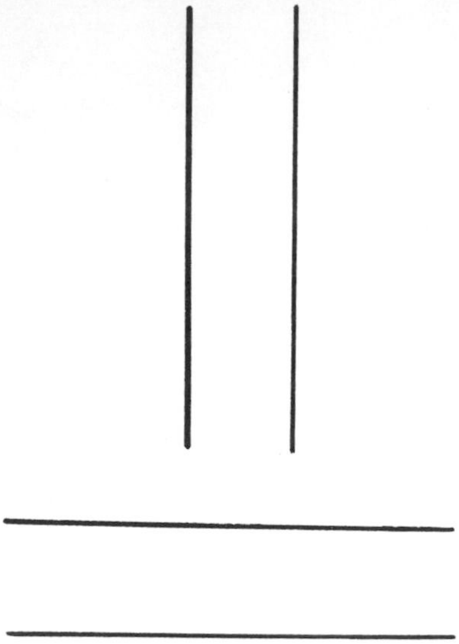

Fig. 2.1   Vertical and horizontal lines.

The Free-Motion Satin Stitch

First, trace or draw onto your material the two vertical and two horizontal lines, as shown in Figure 2.1. Set up your machine for free-motion stitching and load the hoops. (Unless the material is heavy or rather bulky, the hoops will be necessary.) With no foot or ankle in the way, it is simple to place the hoops under the needle. Put the presser bar down and insert the needle at the top of the vertical line. *Walk* the needle for a few stitches by turning the flywheel and gently moving the hoops away from yourself. With the needle *up* add a #2 bight, then lower the needle and slowly push the hoops away from you. This causes you to stitch *toward* yourself.

Step easy on the pedal or employ the reduction gear if your machine has one, for it takes a bit of practice to get the feel of free motion. Are you having difficulty in getting the stitches to "take"? If so, slip a piece of paper under the material. When you reach the end of the vertical line, pull the hoops *toward* you—you are then doing the satin stitch *away* from yourself as you travel up over the very same stitching. This not only teaches you how to travel in the opposite direction, but it fills in the line more, making the satin stitching more pronounced.

Move on to the next vertical line and again insert the needle in the top end of the line. This time as you travel *down*, if you notice a weak spot in the stitching, immediately go back over the weak spot, then proceed on down the line.

Caution: Did you remember to make sure the presser bar was *down* during free-motion stitching? If you forget this, it will be necessary to remove the hoops from the machine. When you turn them over, you will see lots of loops highly resembling tailor tacking. These must be cut away with the embroidery scissors. It may even be necessary to remove the face plate to get rid of the tangles that will occur if you forget to *lower that presser bar.*

The Free-Motion Chain Stitch

Insert the needle in the *left* end of the horizontal line. This time the hoops must be moved to the *left* until the *right* end of the line is reached. If the line isn't thickly covered, merely pull the hoops to the *right;* however, do not turn the hoops around. Stay on the straight line much like the numbers 9 and 3 on a clock. Change the bight to widest and do the other horizontal line. Begin at the *right* end if you wish and pull the hoops *right* in order to cover the line. The two horizontal lines are classic examples of the *chain stitch.*

The Lockstitch

After all this free-motion stitching, it would be a pity to have the threads pull out, so we must provide a simple *lockstitch.*

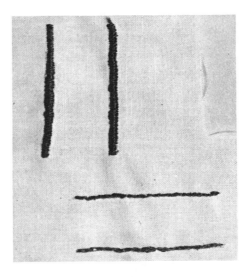

Fig. 2.2 Horizontal and vertical free-motion stitching.

Lockstitch is to free-motion what backstitch is to regular sewing, and is swiftly accomplished by canceling out the bight (with the needle in the *up* position) and sewing about three stationary stitches wherever you plan on clipping the thread. With the needle up, add the bight and proceed to stitch, like you did in the first vertical row.

Now trace one of the patterns shown in Figure 2.3.

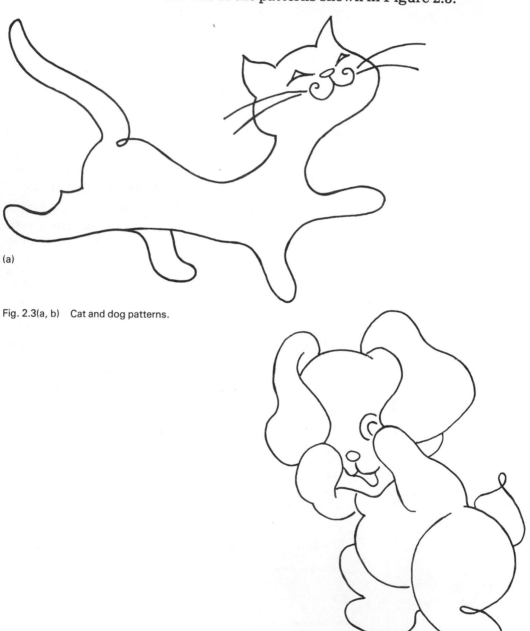

(a)

Fig. 2.3(a, b)   Cat and dog patterns.

(b)

The Free-Motion Linear Stitch

Load the hoops and place them under the bare needle, lowering the presser bar. Cancel out any bight for now, and follow the lines of the drawings just as you did when you used the linear stitch on the potholder in Chapter 1. The only exception is that now you are set up for free-motion stitching. Remember, there is no stitch length, so you must move the hoops to where you must go. After going over all the lines, add a bight and go over the lines again. The lines are now much more pronounced, but as you come to any end, raise the needle, cancel out the bight, and lockstitch those ends.

Practice these drawings and you will have had sufficient practice to be well on the way to more detailed free-motion embroidery.

Free-Motion Writing

Write your signature on your material. Use the same technique on your signature that you used for the free-motion linear stitch. Once you become proficient at embroidering your signa-

Fig. 2.4   Writing a name.

ture, you can label your coat linings, your children's smocks, aprons, blouses, and so forth.

TRACING PICTURES

Many times we can find the picture we want for embroidery in a magazine or book. No one wants to tear out a page; nor is it always practical to go to the library to make use of the overhead projector or to make a photocopy. Alternatives then have to be explored.

ENLARGING AND REDUCING PICTURES

If the picture we want to use is the exact size we need, it is simple enough to trace it just as we did in Chapter 1, but that's not always the case. Therefore we must learn how to enlarge or reduce the size.

THE FOLDING METHOD. By far the simplest way to do this is the folding method. Suppose the picture in the book is 4″ × 6″ but you need an 8″ × 11″. First trace the picture by placing a piece

Fig. 2.5(a, b) Small and large squares.

(a)

(b)

of 4″ × 6″ tracing paper over it. After you have traced the picture, fold the tracing into five folds; first from bottom to top, then side to side. Repeat these until you have made five folds. You will end with the bottom to the top just like the first fold. This should show 32 squares.

Take the 8″ × 11″ paper and fold it the exact way; it will also have 32 squares. Be sure to make good creases wherever you fold, for these are your guidelines.

All you have to do now is to pencil in the picture around the guidelines on the larger paper, just as the tracing shows on the smaller paper.

Suppose the size you need is only 2½″ × 4½″, yet the picture in the magazine or book is 4″ × 6″. Trace with the 4″ × 6″ paper; fold it. Then fold another paper, 2½″ × 4½″, and pencil it in. The finished size is dependent upon the size paper you use.

Whenever it is necessary to use the folding method, it is easier to use tissue paper—not only because it is easier to see through, but because it can be ironed first, folds more easily, and, once folded, the folds can be ironed. Typing paper is hard to crease, especially in the smaller pieces, and if you don't crease the folds sharply, you will get an inaccurate drawing.

Fig. 2.6   Pantograph.

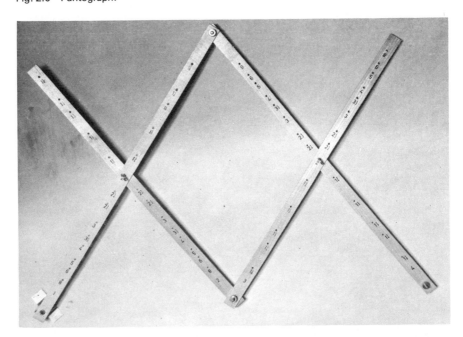

THE GRAPH METHOD. Graph paper comes in different-sized squares. Place the one you are using *under* the magazine picture, and put dressmaker's carbon on top of the graph paper. Place tissue paper *over* the picture, and trace over the picture with a stylus or dried-up ballpoint pen. The tissue paper protects the picture, but this method will transfer well onto the graph paper. Use another size of graph paper to the size you want; if you need the 1″ squares, you can use your cutting board, for there are 1″ squares on most of these.

THE PANTOGRAPH METHOD. You have learned the folding technique and the graph technique. Last, but certainly not least, you should know about a very practical instrument called the *pantograph*. This is an inexpensive tool; and it consists of four bars forming a parallelogram with a foot that can be fastened to the edge of your cutting table much like a vise is attached in the family workshop. The pantograph costs less than $10 and is adjustable for many different ratios. It works for both reductions and enlargements, and you need not be an engineer to use it.

Now that you have learned the basic free-motion technique, you are ready to learn how to create some special effects, which we will discuss in the next chapter.

3 Special Effects

By now you have easily advanced to a point at which you can learn some really special effects that are possible in sewing machine embroidery. We will call the first of these "crewelwork" because of its resemblance to that kind of stitchery. Get ready to start some "needlework" that will be both fun to do and beautiful to look at!

CREWELWORK

In the strict sense of the word, "crewelwork" implies that a kind of worsted yarn or thread has been used for embroidery. Of course we won't use a worsted yarn, but we will use thread and a stitch called the *encroaching stitch;* and the connotation "crewel" always seems to emerge whenever that combination is

used.

To begin, trace the pansy in Figure 3.1 onto your material Butcher linen would be a good fabric to use. If it is your intent to appliqué (apply the finished product to a garment)* the pansy, be sure to *lighten* the pressure. Consult your machine manual if necessary, but generally the lower the number, the lighter the pressure. Usually it is best to work this type of embroidery directly onto the garment rather than to appliqué it; however, the dress shown in Figure 3.3 was appliquéd. This is not advised—but if you wish to try it, cut around the finished pansy and satin stitch it on. If you have not lightened the pressure, you are in trouble. There will be a gap in one of the petals, and you will have to split it open, cut out the parts, then sew it together to get rid of the gap; or you can stuff the gap, and continue satin stitching.

Fig. 3.1 Pansy pattern.

As you trace the pansy, be sure to trace in the directional lines shown, because in using the *encroaching* stitch, which will be described below, it is easy to lose your direction. Set your machine up for free-motion and with the widest bight. Have enough borders on your butcher linen to allow plenty of room to work. You may wish to frame the pansy.

*Appliqué techniques will be discussed in detail in Chapter 5.

Until now we have stayed pretty much with a monochromatic color scheme, but we now must move toward utilizing the tertiary hues. Look at a real pansy or a color picture of one to decide upon the colors you want. For our pansy we will use lavender.

The Encroaching Stitch

Thread up with black thread for the dark areas of the three petals situated near the very center of the pansy. Lay the petal

Fig. 3.2 Pansy done in crewel.

horizontally in order to follow the directional lines, as you did in Chapter 2. Move the hoops slowly and smoothly, slightly rotating them to enable the needle to fill in the area all over that particular part. The stitches are the very adaptable *long and short stitches* and we do not want them to be uniform.

Change to violet-colored thread and fill about one-third of the petal, letting some of the violet run into some of the black. Change the thread to lavender for the next third, blending it into some of the violet. Change the thread to a deeper purple and do the last third. The little overlap can be filled in with purple also, but satin stitch the line separating the overlap from the petal, in order to make it stand out.

This shading and blending is called the *encroaching* stitch, because the long and short stitches encroach upon one another. This technique is used extensively in needle painting. The

Fig. 3.3(a) Long dress.

triangle in the center of the pansy should be filled in with a rust color; the inverted "V" with yellow.

With further practice you will find you will be able to create a roll-edged effect for some petals. You can blend one color in with another in order to make different variations of colors; or make the outer edge of a petal light where it overlaps a petal behind it. It is even possible to blend so well as to give the illusion of a petal contouring either to the left or the right. That is up to the person doing the "needle painting." Using the darker color at the base of a petal helps to effect some semblance of depth in many instances; however, reversing the order of coloring looks good also—i.e., you can "paint" purple, lavender, and violet from the center *out*, rather than in the way we just did.

Often, machine crewelwork can be done using variegated thread, which can be bought anywhere thread is sold. Trace the palm tree in Figure 3.4. Use green variegated thread for the leaves employing the directional technique you learned for

Fig. 3.3(b)   Pansy pillow.

making the pansy. Because you are using variegated thread, you do not have to worry about the shading, for it is all done automatically as it comes off the spool. Turn your hoops in order to follow the directional lines.

Fig. 3.4 Palm tree pattern.

Either a brown thread or variegated brown thread can be used for the trunk. The variegated thread will create the appearance of sunlight hitting the trunk.

Fig. 3.5   Palm tree in variegated thread.

Another special effect possible with sewing machine embroidery is lettering. You will find this an enjoyable and useful technique.

SAMPLERS AND OLD SAWS

In fabric stores you can find patterns for many different samplers. Of course, samplers are usually done in the cross stitch, while "old saws" are done in various types of lettering. Usually the envelope containing the sampler pattern also includes one good alphabet. By buying the one pattern you have both an "old saw" and a sampler to use. The sampler can be finished in the cross stitch that we learned in Chapter 1.

Let us assume you have found a nice-looking alphabet in the children's coloring book and you want to use it to make up a

Fig. 3.6 Old saw.

machine-embroidered "old saw." First decide what you want the saying to be, and on what material. Then decide upon the finishing of the edges. Do the edges first, then trace the lettering from the book with a pencil and tracing paper.

Turn the traced letters *over* and go over the *wrong* side with your transfer pencil. If it is hard to see through the paper, use a lighted makeup mirror, or the window, or sliding glass doors as a tracing surface.

Place the linen in the hoops after you have transferred and properly centered the lettering, and then use any of the setups and techniques you have already learned to stitch the letters. A simple chain stitch or satin stitch will always suffice.

The old saw shown in Figure 3.6 was done on butcher linen. The edge guide was set for 1" and three sides were sewn in 1" from the edge, using a narrow zigzag stitch in matching thread. This secured the inner threads. After you have finished your lettering, use a seam ripper to remove the *crosswise* threads from the *bottom* of the saying within the 1" edge of the linen. Remove the *lengthwise* threads from both sides from within the 1" edge. This makes a nice fringe. You can place a rod inside the seam at the top of your embroidery piece; then tie some braid or cord to both ends of the rod in order to hang up your "old saw."

SOME SPECIAL STITCHES

Think of all the marvelous things you can now do with the co-operation of your wonderful zigzag machine. By now you have learned many varieties, but there are more. When you know lots of stitches, you can pick and choose from them for special effects before you start on a project. Here are a number of special stitches you can learn.

The Stem Stitch

Trace the leaf in Figure 3.7, making sure to trace in the directional lines. Set the bight on #4 and use the horizontal stitch for the filling-in. Go from one end of the line and back over again, keeping the hoops moving smoothly, going right along without clipping threads. Follow the line directions and take your time. This kind of special stitching is best done if you move slowly, letting the machine do the hurrying. When you reach the tip, turn the hoops slowly to make the transition from one direction to the other.

To do the vein of the leaf use a #2 bight in the horizontal position. The vein will then show a tiny chain stitch. Of course if your machine has the chain stitch built in, simply use it.

The stem of the leaf is worked on both sides of the line; the stitches are made up of tiny chain stitches with a slight backward and forward movement with the hoops. When both a thick and thin appearance is needed, slide around any curves instead of turning the hoops.

Fig. 3.7   Leaf with directional lines and a stem-stitch drawing.

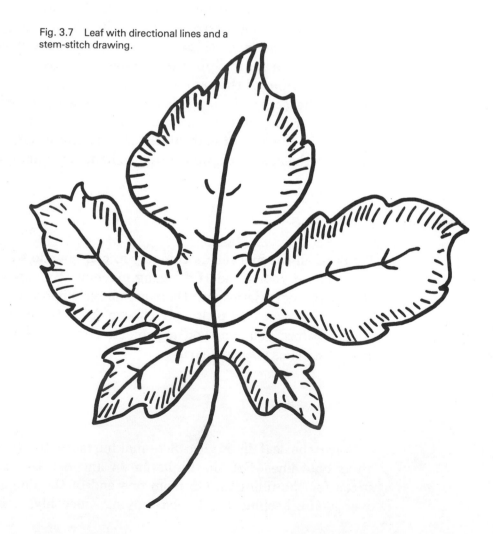

Fig. 3.8   Finished directional leaf with stem stitch.

The Cordstitch

Trace the holly leaf in Figure 3.9—holly is a good leaf to out-line with cord. Hold a spool of button and carpet thread in your lap. To secure the end of the cord, loop the end around the machine needle and give it a good lockstitch to hold the cord. Set the bight just wide enough to cover the cord, then zigzag

Fig. 3.9   Holly leaf pattern.

Fig. 3.10   Corded holly leaf.

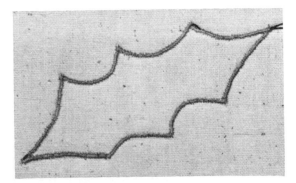

over the cord, pausing to place it properly along the outline of the holly leaf.

If you feel you are not expert enough to cordstitch this way, you have an alternative technique. Set up for automatic, attach the raised seam-presser foot with its cord guide, and follow the outline. Hold the cord straight up. This will not only keep it out of your way so that you can see the outline of the holly leaf, it will also make a smoother cordstitch.

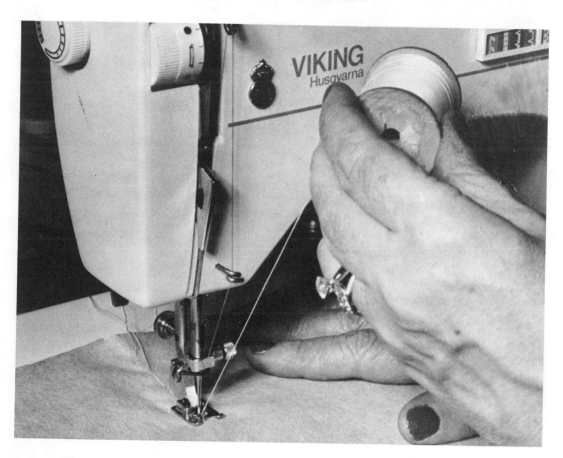

Fig. 3.11   Presser foot—proper way to hold cord.

To further practice cordstitching, trace the fried egg pot-holder design in Figure 3.12. Cut the yolk from a yellow or gold scrap of cotton, the next part in white, and any background color for the base. Place the appliqué on the potholder by temporarily holding it in place with a *bartack*. A bartack is made by using a bight but no length, no feed dogs allowed. In some appliqués the raw edges are ironed under; however, by using the cordstitch you can eliminate the need for ironing, because you will be covering the raw edges with a wide zigzag and cord. Use a cord of the color and thickness desired, do not forget to lock-stitch, then finish the potholder as you learned in Chapter 1.

Fig. 3.12   Potholder pattern (fried egg).

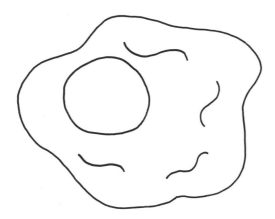

Fig. 3.13   Fried egg potholder in cordstitch appliqué.

Daisies are probably the most popular flowers in embroidery. They are seen in transfer patterns everywhere, so it is well to learn how to stitch both the large daisies and the small ones.

First, trace a circle around a dime and fit several daisy petals into the circle. Set the bight on wide and *bartack* from the center to the outer end of the petal and back again three or four times. Try to end at the center of the flower (not the center of the petal) for neater daisies, and when all the petals have been done by using the bartack technique, continue around the circle in lock-stitch. The tiny daisies will then show no loose ends or cuttings, and will never rip out.

Fig. 3.14   Bartacked daisies.

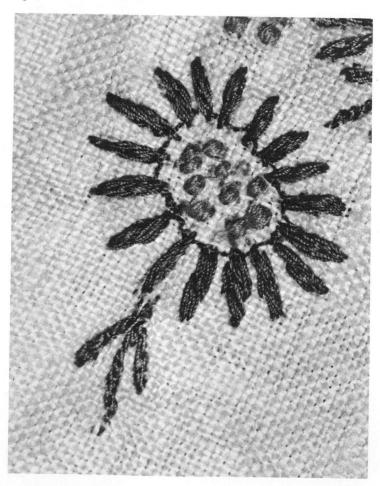

Large daisies are very smart-looking when they have been filled in with a good thick satin stitch, and the smartest way to do this is by engaging the versatility of the bight. Trace the drawing in Figure 3.15, drawing several daisies. In this draw-

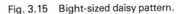

Fig. 3.15 Bight-sized daisy pattern.

Fig. 3.16 Bight-sized daisy.

ing, just to make it easier, the widest part does not exceed the widest bight of the average machine. In this instance a #4 bight was used. Some machines can go wider, however. In reality this is a very uniform satin stitch, but to make it look attractive, you will need some dexterity, because your right hand must regulate the bight while your left must move the hoops.

Using the free-motion technique, set the bight on #1 and begin at the narrow end of the petal. As you move along, watch the outer lines of the petal so you will know just when you should increase or decrease the bight. If the first few you do in this way look like rolling pins, don't despair—this is a common problem. Just keep a sharp eye on when to change the bight. You know you have reached the summit once your widest part is made, so you simply begin decreasing the bight until the other end is reached. You might call these your "bight-size daisies."

French Knots (Seed Stitches)

French knots (or seed stitches) always seem to go right along with daisies, so set the bight on #1 or #1½. Shoot several small stitches one on top of the other as you learned in lockstitch. The tiny bight makes a very small raised spot if you do this while the needle is in a stationary position.

Raise the needle and shift to the next place you want to make another French knot, but *slacken* the thread about 2 or 3 inches each time you jump from one French knot to another. In French knots the lockstitch is automatically in effect; you have merely stayed in the same place longer, in order to *raise* a knot. In the lockstitch you have no bight and you shoot only three times. The French knots will take about ten or twelve shots.

Once all the knots are completed, take all the *slack* thread and, holding it taut, clip it short. If you forgot to leave the slack it will be almost impossible to get rid of the thread ends where you jumped from one knot to the next one.

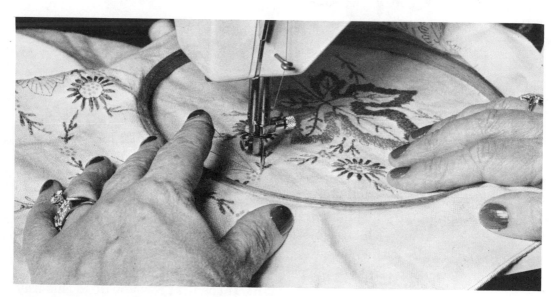

Fig. 3.17   French knots showing slackening of the thread.

The Darning Stitch

Draw a circle of loops onto your scrap material, as shown in Figure 3.18. Remember the free-motion linear stitch you did in Chapter 2? Using that, go over and over the motif. This is simply another way of filling in, and is often referred to as the *darning stitch*. The proper way to manage the hoops in this type of filling in is to tilt the hoops back and forth as though you were panning for gold.

Draw or trace a circle the size of a quarter and set the bight on #4. Following the rules of the horizontal line, fill in the circle. Draw another circle and fill it in to look like the design on the baby rompers in Figure 3.20, on which a cat is sitting by a ball. Do you see the two very definite lines about one-third and two-thirds down the ball? These are really not lines at all. The ball was turned around so the sewer could work horizontally; a #4

Fig. 3.18   Loop pattern.

Fig. 3.19   Finished loops.

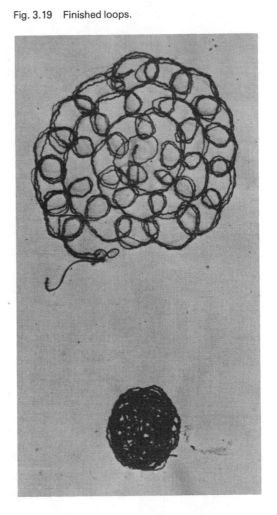

bight was used to fill in about one-third of the way with one color, then the color was changed for the next part, with a small space left between colors. The last third of the ball was done in the same color as the first third, again with a small space left. The contrast in color gives the stitching more personality with two definite lines. These lines are actually a non-line.

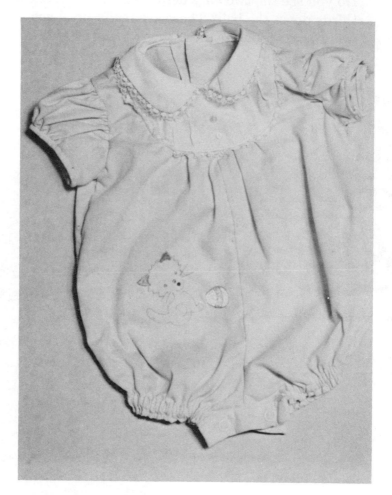

Fig. 3.20 Finished rompers.

The Stroke Stitch

Draw some geometric designs like the ones in Figure 3.21. Using the reduction gear and free motion with a #1½ bight, put your right hand on the flywheel and make one stitch. With the material taut in the hoops, move the hoops with your left hand and the flywheel with your right hand so that the thread can be brought over to the other side of the drawing with *no* stitches being made in between. The #1½ bight is necessary in order to secure the thread on either side of the motif. You use the fly-wheel to help you get the needle right on target when you try to reach the other side, where you again give the one stitch in order to secure· the thread. Repeat back and forth until it becomes easy—this is the *stroke stitch,* and is one of the more important stitches you will learn.

Fig. 3.21   Geometric drawings.

The Flat Embroidery Stitch

This is another stitch that is important. It consists of filling in a motif with a series of *stroke* stitches after having first outlined the motif with linear stitching. You then turn the hoops so that the motif is lying horizontally, then stroke stitch *across* the motif (toward yourself and away from yourself) to superimpose several threads in order to cover the motif. Lockstitch.

Fig. 3.22   Pattern for both flat embroidery and padded satin stitch.

The Padded Satin Stitch

Using the same motif pattern, draw it onto your material and outline it in order to strengthen the edges. Again turn the hoops so that the motif is lying horizontally and do the linear stitch

Fig. 3.23　Flat embroidery.

Fig. 3.24　Padded satin stitch.

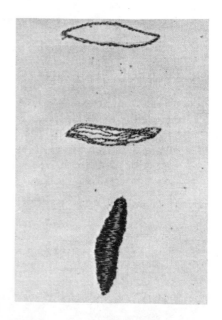

inside the motif, moving the hoops left and right only. Once that is done, turn it to the *vertical* position, and using the bight in order to taper (as in the bight-sized daisy), go over the whole motif. This technique is called the *padded satin stitch*.

Fig. 3.25   Bouquet wall plaque.

These last new stitches you have just mastered certainly have their place, for they add a great deal of interest and even texture to a design. As in the wall plaque, for which we stuffed parts of the design and thereby gave it a three-dimensional effect, we can also make special effects by using these different stitches. If the satin stitch is used too often in one article to the exclusion of the many other kinds of stitches, the article will have a monotonous look. Using many kinds of stitches is fun to do and makes for clever and interesting pieces of embroidery.

Fig. 3.26   Brushed denim shirt showing front (a) and back (b).

(a)   (b)

4 Special Materials

HEAVY FABRICS

You may have assumed, up to now, that you can only use sewing machine embroidery on the lighter fabrics. This is not so. There are many things you can do, using your machine and your imagination, to beautify things like towels, felt skirts, holiday tablecloths, and even bedspreads. In the first part of this chapter we will see how. Later we will discuss other types of materials, including the many threads and yarns you can use.

A bathmat placed over the bathtub with the initial of the family name; washcloths with tiny hands or flowers; bath towels with "His & Hers"—all of these personalized accessories can be done with your own sewing machine.

Every embroiderer needs plenty of patterns of many different types, with alphabets, designs, and monograms. In embroidering heavy materials like towels, however, you cannot iron these on, so you must either trace your iron-on transfers face-up or use lettering that is not from a package of transfers.

How do we transfer lettering to velour and cotton terrycloth when it stands to reason that this is going to be difficult on cloth with all those little loops? Pick out initials that are fairly large (4 or 6 inches), because they will look better and be easier to transfer. Trace these with a regular pencil on to some heavy waxed paper, such as that used to wrap meats. This comes in a box resembling a facial tissue box, and your butcher uses it all the time. Of course we do not reverse the lettering, because we will be working on towelling, face-up.

Trace the initials onto the special paper, then take a ruler or anything that will serve the purpose (maybe the edge of a notebook) and draw four lines around the sides of the initial, touching the farthest points. Centering is done this way whether an initial, monogram, or a picture is to be transferred. Bring both vertical lines together and crease the paper; open it up and

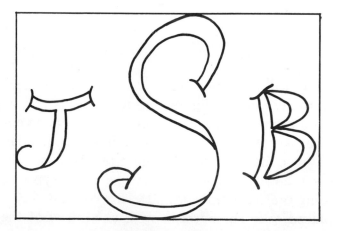

Fig. 4.1   How to center a monogram.

bring the two horizontal lines together and crease it again. Where the two lines cross in the center *is* the center. It is this mark that must be placed over the center of the article being stitched.

60

In the case of a bath towel, decide how far up from the edge you want to place the initials, then locate its true center by folding the towel lengthwise. Put the two centers together (on the pattern and the towel) and the initials will be absolutely centered.

To center a bathmat, you must fold it both lengthwise and crosswise, pin the center of the bathmat to mark it, then unfold it and pin the pattern on. Now everything should be centered, if you followed the directions correctly.

THE EMBROIDERY SPRING

We would now be ready to sew, except that the bobbin thread will almost always have difficulty in catching the top thread when we are using this type of material, so we must use an embroidery or darning spring.

Fig. 4.2   Embroidery spring and needle.

In free-motion stitching we are working with a bare needle anyway, so it is little or no trouble at all to attach this spring. It will hold down the terrycloth, giving the needle and bobbin a chance to catch the thread. This spring also prevents your skipping stitches on towelling and other thicker materials. Put the embroidery spring over the needle-bar screw, insert the needle into the initial on the waxed paper, and, using any stitch you prefer, outline the initial. Remove the paper before doing the fill-in, for it has done its job once the pattern is outlined onto the material.

The little embroidery spring will bounce along like a jogger, and enable you to do a trim job. If some of the paper fails to come out, don't worry—it will all come out in the wash.

Fig. 4.3 "N" and "R" initial towels.

THE VIBRATOR SHOE TECHNIQUE

If you have ever done darning on your zigzag machine, you may prefer to use the vibrator instead of investing in the embroidery spring. Remember when you were learning to insert the hoops under the needle while the foot was still on? Refer to Chapter 1, and put your machine on the "vibrator control." Also attach the darning shoe that comes with your machine in the accessory box. The shoe arm does not go over the needle-bar screw as the embroidery spring did; rather, you allow it to roam free. Any time we engage the vibrator we do not have pressure or tension. The presser bar becomes useless, so forget it. The tension means absolutely nothing, and this is the only time you may set your tension at the highest without its mattering. So you can set it way up to #10. Use the vibrator in the same manner as the embroidery spring: the only difference is that you set it up as just explained.

Fig. 4.4   Darning shoe under needle.

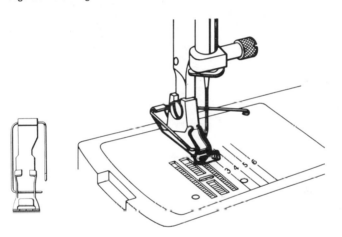

If you like your monogram or initial appliquéd to the towels, buy washable white satin, use gold-colored thread, and use the satin in place of the steak paper. All the work is done on the satin on the towel. Once the initial is done, go all around the outside edges of the motif with a narrow satin stitch, using the automatic setup. With the embroidery scissors cut away the excess satin, then cover up all the outside edges with a wider satin stitch. This not only gives a smooth, even appearance, but prevents the satin from raveling as well. The towel showing an "M" in Figure 4.5 was done in this way. If you appliqué a motif onto a towel using material that does not ravel, such as pellon, you can trace the pattern onto the pellon. Do all the work on the pellon on the towel, but you do not have to do the outer edges as you did when you used the satin. Do the edges once with a #2½ bight, then cut away the excess pellon. This technique was used in doing the Christmas motif on the hand towel shown in Figure 4.5. All other towel work was done using the heavy paper.

(a)

Fig. 4.5(a) Satin-appliquéd towel, burp bib, and
Christmas motif; (b) His, Hers, Heirs.

(b)

IRON-ON PATCHES: MAKING YOUR OWN

Iron-on patches are generally used on heavier materials—in part because they require a very hot temperature to set and also because most of them are more appropriate to the heavier-textured items. Iron-on patches are very popular today, but like everything else, they cost too much! If you make your own, the cost is negligible, for it takes very little thread, and an imaginative patch can be made from scraps. The transfer patterns bought from the fabric store are great, but for practice let's use the tomato pattern from Figure 4.6.

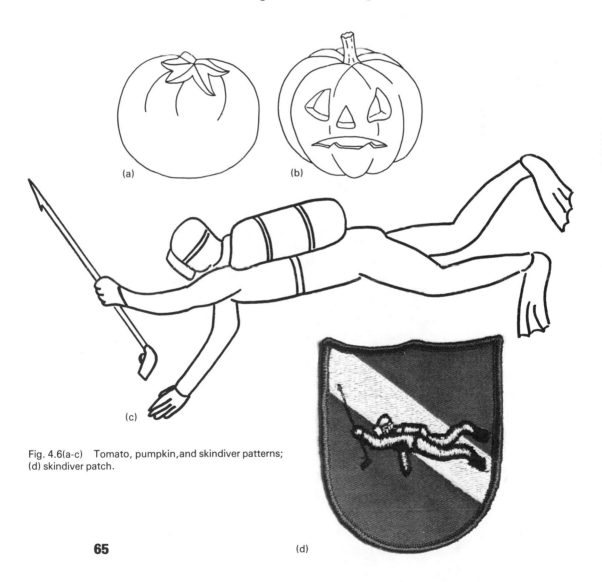

Fig. 4.6(a-c)   Tomato, pumpkin, and skindiver patterns; (d) skindiver patch.

The tomato works up well if you use a red twill with a green thread. The leaf should be worked the same way as the one you read about in Chapter 3. Do the stem, then decide whether you plan to apply the patch directly to the garment, or finish it and use it later.

If you want to finish the patch for later application, refer to Chapter 1 and set your machine up for scallops. Set the bight on wide, and go all around the tomato. Clip the threads, then iron on a backing of scraps from nonwoven interfacing. This not only gives a good body to the patch—it also seals in any thread ends. (Buy the iron-on interfacing that has adhesive on one side only.) When you apply this patch, use the zipper foot and regular sewing, and stay close to the satin stitching. The patch can easily be removed in whole later on if desired.

Fig. 4.7   Tomato.

If you plan on attaching the patch as soon as you have done the embroidery on it (using the green thread), cut out the tomato and also a piece of Stitchwitchery (this has adhesive on both sides) and iron it onto the garment. After it cools, set up for automatic and then do the satin stitch around it. It is now on permanently.

To do the pumpkin, trace the pattern onto yellow or gold material and outline it in either brown or black thread.

OVALS AND CIRCLES. So many patches are oval-shaped; you could start by tracing the oval opening from a box of facial tissues, an oval casserole, or a large roaster. For circles, trace thimbles, coins, cups, saucers, dinner plates, or large canning kettles. Reproduce any size you need.

Perfect circles on the machine can be done with plain stitches or cam stitches. Set your machine for automatic and put your hoops on. Remember the quilting bar? If you have a hole in the end of the bar, fine. If not, there is another attachment (the circle bar) that resembles the quilting bar, except that it is much longer, and there is a hole in the shorter end.

Fig. 4.8   Circle bar in hoops.

Figure out where you want the center of the circle to be, then tape a thumbtack to the wrong side of the material so the sharp point comes through to the right side. Place the attachment through the needle shank with the hole in the attachment over the thumbtack. Tighten the screw in the needle bar, step on the pedal, and whiz away. You will make a perfect circle every time with no effort. Get fancier, and use a cam to further enhance the circle.

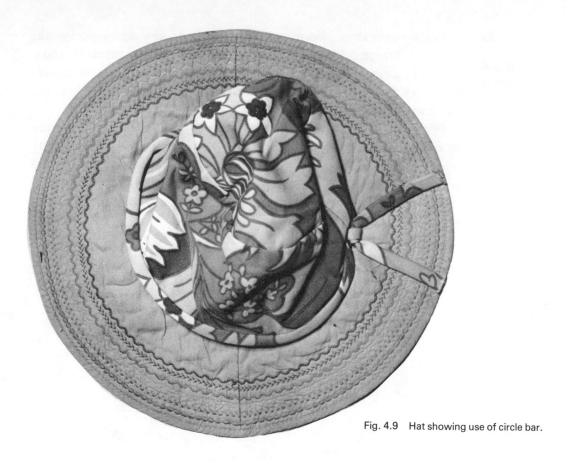

Fig. 4.9   Hat showing use of circle bar.

Now you not only know how to make tiny and medium-sized circles as in the flower stitcher, but others as well.

ROUND BEDSPREADS.   Owners of circular beds know that a round bedspread is almost always very expensive. So while we are on the subject of circles, let's consider the person who owns a 7-foot circular bed. Here you can realize a huge savings by just using the floor: if you have any floors with the 9 inch tile squares, you have a built-in pattern for the top or fancywork part of the bedspread. Draw the pattern right on the floor tiles by counting down five tiles: then counting five tiles to the right, stopping just 3 inches short of the two end tiles involved. Tie a 42 inch string to a pencil, place the end of the string at the angle, and have a friend stand on it. With the pencil, begin at one of the end tiles and draw on to the other end tile. A perfect quarter of a circle pattern results. Use newspaper taped together for your pattern if you wish.

68

TABLECLOTHS AND CHRISTMAS-TREE SKIRTS. Every autumn as we bring in the tablecloths from the umbrella tables and pack away the lawn furniture for the year, wouldn't it be wise to not only make up some terrycloth tablecloths for next summer but also to make a Christmas-tree skirt, using the same pattern? The tablecloth could be embroidered using the towel technique described earlier in this chapter. The tree skirt could be cut from felt (and therefore would not require a hem). Felt does not have to be put into hoops, and if you use the holly leaf pattern from Chapter 3 with other Christmas motifs, a very inexpensive tree skirt can be made.

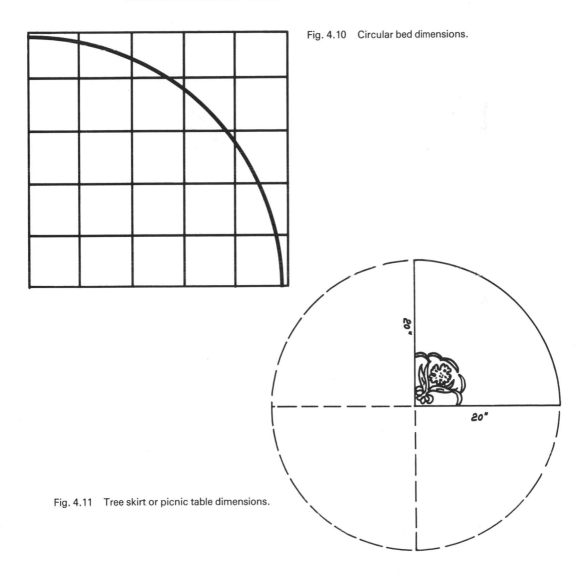

Fig. 4.10   Circular bed dimensions.

Fig. 4.11   Tree skirt or picnic table dimensions.

Among what we have called "special materials" we must include the lighter fabrics. Some of these will be discussed in Chapter 5 (sweater material, tricots, etc.). Nylon net lends itself well to machine-embroidery work—it can be used alone or combined with other materials.

TECHNIQUES

In working with this material, it is well to first make a simple round doily. Trace the pattern in Figure 4.12, turn it, and repeat to complete the circle. A coarse tulle or net is best, and the nylon bridal veiling with hexagonal meshes is just right. Use nylon thread both in the bobbin and in the needle—and if there ever was a place where you should stick to matching colors of thread, this is it. Any setup and any stitch can be done with this durable net and durable nylon thread. Use the hoops.

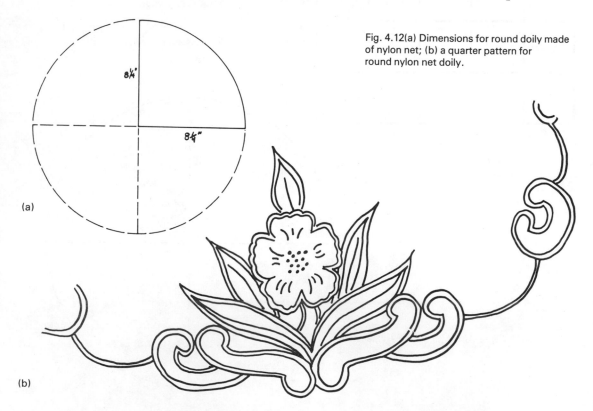

Fig. 4.12(a) Dimensions for round doily made of nylon net; (b) a quarter pattern for round nylon net doily.

(a)

(b)

Trace your pattern on tissue paper and slip the tissue paper under the nylon net. This serves a dual purpose; it stabilizes the net, much as typing paper does for other light materials; and at the same time it lets you see the pattern very clearly. Because net does not run, fray, or tear you don't have to bind its edges. Nylon net is so easy to work on it is almost impossible to tell the difference between the right and wrong side of the work.

Fig. 4.13   Nylon net embroidery.

Try combining nylon net with other materials. Trace the pattern in Figure 4.14 onto a piece of light cotton. Use all matching colors, and set the machine up for automatic satin stitch. First do the three petals between the diamond shapes, using the large tapered daisy technique from Chapter 3. Next do the diamond shape in a wide satin stitch, never varying the width. Now do the scrolls on either side, using the same tapering technique (Chapter 3) and swinging from the smallest to the largest bight. Clean up all the threads, then cut out the centers of the diamond and outer scrolls. Using scrap pieces of nylon net in matching color, lay the net either over or under the cutout places and stitch in place with a small zigzag. Because it is

71

possible to see through the net, some people prefer to sew it from the right side; others prefer the wrong side. At any rate, the zigzag stitch will not only hold the net in place to enhance the embroidery; it will also prevent any fraying of the cotton material. Cut away the excess net.

Fig. 4.14 Pattern for sleeve insert.

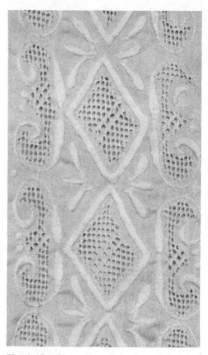

Fig. 4.15   Sleeve insert made with net.

The pattern just finished would look well embroidered on the sleeves of a shirt, as in Figures 4.14 and 4.15.

Identify this type of embroidery (since it consists of thousands of tiny hexagons) as "mille net"—for *mille* means thousand.

SPECIAL THREADS

Within the category of "special materials" comes the use of special "threads"—and this includes yarnwork, metallic threads, braiding, and so forth. As we discuss these various types of filaments that may be used in your creative sewing machine embroidery, we will also continue to illustrate and describe various stitch combinations that will enhance the beauty and special look of your handiwork.

Yarnwork Stitching

Treadle owners can join in on yarnwork. For this we use the free-motion setup with transparent thread in the needle. Ask your fabric store for nylon transparent thread. It comes in regular spools and quickly adapts itself to whatever color it is being used on.

With the transparent thread in the needle and scrap thread in the bobbin, using the free-motion setup, *tighten* the tension to #2. This is just a bit looser than the automatic setup. Trace the sunflower in Figure 4.16. Make the tracing rather large in order to make the first yarnwork easier. We won't be using hoops, and as you know the length of the stitch is up to you in free-motion, so plan on pushing the material along using longer intervals on the straight and shorter intervals on curves. Keep the stitching close to the inner edges in order to avoid a squashed, matted effect.

Fig. 4.16 Sunflower pattern.

Beginning with one of the petals, lay the yarn you have selected down and lockstitch the end. Proceed on the inner edge of the yarn, keeping it on the line of the petal, using the embroidery scissors. Each time it is necessary to keep the yarn in line, be sure to keep the needle in, as in pivoting. Keep going until you come to the starting point, then lockstitch. If you want to completely fill in the petals and shade them at the same time, take some other weight and color, and repeat. Any kind of yarn can be used. You can also just keep going with the yarn you began with, until all the petals are filled. Lockstitch an additional piece of yarn on, if you run out of yarn. Change yarn color and do the stem and leaves, leaving the center of the flower until later.

Isn't it great that although you change yarn colors, you do not have to bother changing the thread? Think of the time you will save when you are doing a large bouquet with dozens of colors.

Bouclé

Any thread can be used for bouclé, because it doesn't show through. Bouclé is a nubby yarnwork that looks good for flower centers (especially sunflowers) and for trim on wool clothing. Use six strands of yarn about a yard long and loop the end by

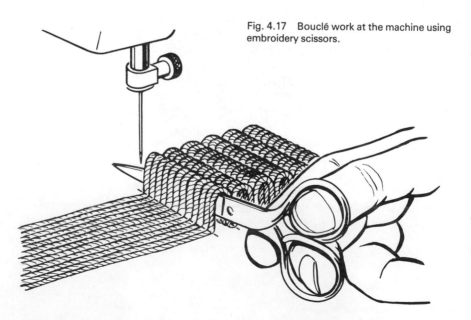

Fig. 4.17 Bouclé work at the machine using embroidery scissors.

free-motion across the yarns and back again. Leaving the needle in, put your embroidery scissors under the layers of yarn and pull to the right. Sew across and back again, repeating this procedure until the proper amount of loops are made. If you want tall loops, pull higher as you pull to the right. If you want them small and nubby, pull very little. The best nubby appearance you can get is by using the embroidery scissors; the size is then easy to control.

To add bouclé to a sleeve of a ready-made dress, put the sleeve over the free arm of the machine and work your free-motion stitches.

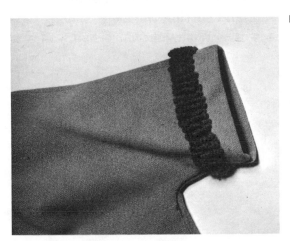

Fig. 4.18 Dress sleeve with bouclé.

The Twist

Now let's fill in the center of the yarn flower with bouclé. Let's also make it multicolor. Gather six strands of yarn as before, except this time each one should be a different color and only as long as you can reach with your right arm. Place the strands side by side and secure the ends with scotch tape. Fasten this end to the flywheel of your machine with the tape, unthread the needle, and place your needle-sharpening pad under the needle, lowering the presser bar. With your right hand, gently pull the yarn to your right as far as you can reach. You measured your yarn this way, remember? Step on the pedal and let the flywheel create the most perfect multicolored twist you ever saw, and all in the exact order you laid the yarn in to begin with. The striped pattern is repeated to perfection for as long as the length of the yarn.

For a larger twist, hold the yarns with little or no pull; for a tight, smaller twist, pull taut. Pull extremely taut if you prefer a striped elastic-type twist, but before letting up on the grip of both ends of any newly made twist, be sure to fasten them temporarily with scotch tape, or your twist will uncoil. Thread the machine (using the newly sharpened needle) and sew across both ends. In this way the twist will stay in shape. With embroidery scissors, even the ends if necessary.

With this yarn, return to the center of your flower and using the bouclé technique, fill in the center. If you prefer a more bushy center, pull your yarn to the right about 2 inches. Once the center is all filled in, take the scissors and taper it, leaving the center tall, and cutting the loops shorter close to the outer edges of the center. With your hairbrush, you can give it a good brushing.

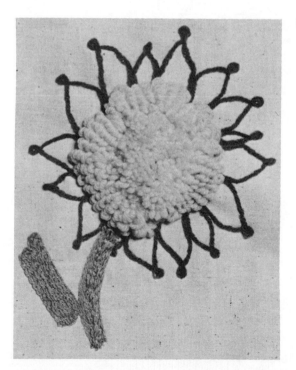

Fig. 4.19   Sunflower.

Fringe

There is a sewing aid called a "weaver's reed" that fits all machines. It is used with regular setup and a straight stitch with the regular foot. To use this, wind the yarn around the reed; do not be too particular about layering it tightly up against the preceding rows; just wind along and every once in awhile push the whole works up toward the end of the reed. Once the reed is filled so that no more yarn can be wound on it, place the reed under the needle with the slot to the right and sew down the slot. Upon reaching the end of the slot, push the far end's lock open, and push away the yarn that has been sewed. Keep on winding more yarn until you have the length you wish. Once you have enough, take the scissors and cut through the loops—and there is your automatic fringe. If you need a much wider fringe, tape on an extension of cardboard to the left side of the reed.

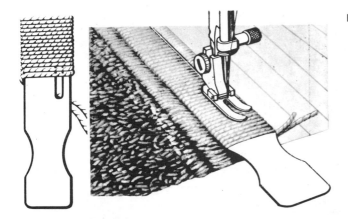

Fig. 4.20   Weaver's reed and machine.

Fig. 4.21   Pillow showing fringe.

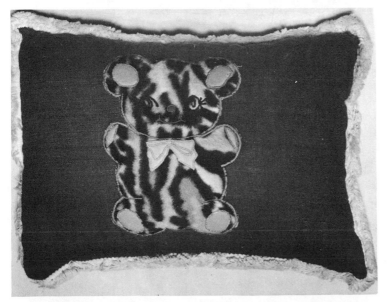

There are spools of metallic and other threads on the market today that can be used in the same manner as ordinary thread. Then there are spools or cones of fancy heavier thread that must necessarily be wound by hand onto the bobbin. In *couching,* our goal is to lay a heavier thread upon the good side of the garment and catch it at intervals with matching thread.

Trace the pattern in Figure 4.23; hand-wind some fancy thread onto the bobbin with matching color (not texture) in the needle. Set your machine up for automatic and zigzag stitch that is just wide enough to hold the fancy thread intact. A stitch length of 2 would be a good length.

Fig. 4.22 Couching work taken from the superchain stitch blouse.

The pattern should be placed on the wrong side of the garment, and all work done from the wrong side. At any beginning or at any ending (wherever you plan to clip) you must hand-tie the ends. This is done by a change of tension. Flip the tension to its highest number; place the left index finger on the needle thread, and with the right hand move the flywheel a turn or two. This will bring up the fancy thread from the right side of the garment and through to the wrong side, enabling you to tie a knot. Clip all excess thread ends.

Fig. 4.23 Couching pattern.

If the thread you wish to use can go through a needle, you can handle it in the same way as cord stitch, but any thread too heavy for the needle can still be applied, using the *couching* method. Some time ago metallic (silver or gold) thread came on large cones and if you wanted to use them on the machine, it was necessary to wind them onto the bobbin and put the *bobbin* on the spool holder, with a spool of thread on top of this to hold the bobbin down. It was much easier to use the couching method. Now the thread comes in spools and can be used through the needle or bobbin. The metallic thread will even work well using a cam design.

Soutache

Soutache is a narrow braid used for trimming. It can be purchased in most any store. It can also be made on your machine if you use the *twist* technique. With the machine set for regular stitching and the straight stitch, thread up with matching thread for the braid. Attach the braiding foot. The braiding attach-

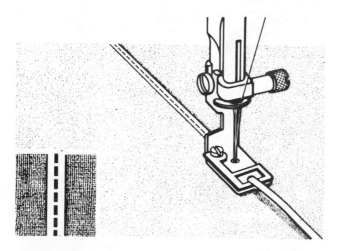

Fig. 4.24   Braiding foot.

ment is one of the most fabulous inventions, because soutache is very popular. With the help of the braiding foot we can make our own *passementerie* (heavy embroideries or edgings). Holding the braid in your lap, feed it into the hole of the braiding foot, and with a long stitch length for straight lines and a short stitch length for the curves, use matching thread and sew away with no effort. You cannot possibly miss on stitching the braid, for that is well taken care of by the attachment. The only thing you have to do is keep your eye on the lines of the pattern.

Unlike couching, braiding is done from the right side. Because the braid is narrow, it is difficult to fold it under to hide the ends, so stab a hole in the fabric with the seam ripper and push the end of the braid through the hole with it, allowing quarter-inch ends on the wrong side of the garment. Make a bartack to hold the ends, and later clip away any excess braid from the wrong side. If your design can possibly end in a seam line, you simply enclose the end in the seam. Cowboy shirts very often use lots of soutache (for example, a cowboy roping a steer—the soutache is the rope).

Passementerie

Suppose you want a good trim around the ends of the sleeves in a blouse or around the edges of a jacket. So often the trim is what makes the jacket. You can buy trim ½" wide and stitch it on, or you can use the braiding technique, laying the braid side by side until the ½" width is reached. This, combined with other trim, makes an elegant appearance.

The Superchain Stitch

On some machines there is a built-in chain stitch that goes much farther than the chain stitch you learned in Chapter 2. In this *superchain stitch*, the pattern is drawn on the wrong side and you work from the wrong side. This is the time when we remove the bobbin and use only the needle thread. If you want larger loops of chain stitch, loosen the tension; for smaller loops, tighten the tension. If you have ever opened a sugar sack, you know how swiftly a chain stitch can be removed. So fasten every end everywhere on the chain stitch.

The blouse or shirt jacket in Figure 4.25 contains the couching, soutache, and passementerie stitches. The button loops were made by the twist; the smaller curves were done by couching, the larger work by the superchain stitch, and the passementerie around all the edges is a half-inch braid applied by stitching in the ditch with the zipper foot on.

Fig. 4.25   Superchain stitch on blouse.

This concludes our long chapter on special materials and threads. Now we will describe some more methods of machine embroidery so you can add to your repertoire of beautiful stitches.

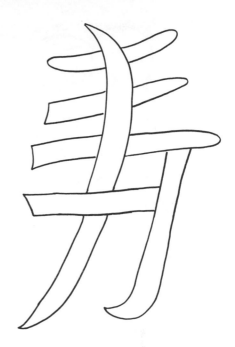

5 More Fancywork

Are you ready for more embroidery fun? In this chapter we will describe several new ways of special embroidering using your sewing machine. First we'll look at various types of appliquéing which we have already mentioned several times. You will find that many of the techniques are by now familiar to you, so thread up your machine and get sewing!

APPLIQUÉING

To begin, enlarge and trace one of the furry animals in Figure 5.1. Decide whether you want a stuffed toy, a pillow, or elbow and knee protectors.

Fig. 5.1(a,b) Furry animals patterns.

(a)

(b)

84

REVERSE APPLIQUÉ

To make the pillow, you must select material that is suitable for the front of the pillow, even though we refer to it here as a backing.

Center the backing material just as you centered the bathmat. With the wrong side of the backing toward you and the paper pattern face up, center the pattern to the backing. Pin with a safety pin. Place a piece of fake fur with the good side down on the table. Put the centered piece onto the wrong side of the fur. Secure it with safety pins. Hoops will not be necessary because of the weight of the fabric.

The needle and the bobbin thread should match in color. Use the free-motion or vibrator setup. Set the bight for #4 and zigzag around the outside edges. This time, instead of using a reduced rate of speed, you will find that the faster the speed is, the better. Do no inside stitching; just do the outline.

Once the outline has been done, remove the material from the machine, turn to the right side, and cut away the excess fur close to the stitching, leaving the pattern intact.

REVERSE EMBROIDERY

Now, with the pattern side toward you once again, embroider the detail work such as under the chin, mouth, and eyes. If you want to appliqué the detail work rather than embroider it, place the proper material next to the machine bed and appliqué; or you can machine-sew buttons on for the eyes, or glue on plastic ones. Once the detail work is done, remove the paper pattern and cut any threads to tidy up. Turn the fur to its right side, and using a wide satin stitch, go all around the outline of the animal again. This time around, you are doing most of the sewing into the backing material, so use the automatic setup and the automatic satin stitch. Finish the pillow in any way you wish.

For the protectors and the stuffed toy, the pattern must be reversed. The detail work on the front of the stuffed toy should be done first, by reverse embroidery; then the two pieces should be placed together fur side out. Using an embroidery spring or vibrator shoe, follow the outline of the animal with the satin stitch. Leave a small opening for stuffing.

For the arm or leg protectors, the backing is the good side of the sleeve or leg. Embroider the detail work first (on elbows we show the back of the bear appliqué, on knees, its front) if any, then follow the rules for the pillow. After the elbow or knee protectors are on, sew up the sleeves (or the trouser legs).

SWEATERS. If a sweater is rather tightly knit, embroidery or appliqué can be done on the right side. If the sweater is a very loosely knitted one, trace your pattern on a piece of nylon

Fig. 5.2   Jacket with elbow protectors.

Fig. 5.3   Firm sweater and stretchy sweater.

tricot. Pin the nylon tricot, with pattern face-up, onto the wrong side of the sweater. Use the reverse embroidery technique. If the nylon tricot allows too much give and you find you need more stability, trace your pattern on a piece of lawn material. Lawn is crisper than voile, but not as crisp as organdy, which makes it perfect on extremely stretchy, loose sweaters. Cut away the excess material from the inside of the sweater, after the embroidery has been completed.

Fig. 5.4 Sheer appliqué on a pillowcase and an initaled pillowcase.

SHEER APPLIQUÉ

In sheer appliqué we first must decide whether the article or garment we plan to appliqué is permapress material or not. If it is permapress, the sheer material for the appliqué must be able to withstand the washer and dryer, but not necessarily the iron. Nylon organdy makes a fine sheer material. Many people want their pillowcases heavily adorned with embroidery, while others want very little, for the embroidery may irritate the face. So you can adorn it heavily on one side for looks, and before going to sleep merely turn the pillow over. Figure 5.4 shows a personalized pillowcase done in padded satin stitch, and another with embroidered flowers and sheer appliqué.

Trace your motif onto the nylon organdy and pin it to a pillowcase. Before placing it in the hoops, turn the case wrong side out. This will prevent your inadvertently sewing the opening together, and with the pinned motif prominently showing, there is no chance of sewing on the wrong side.

Do all the embroidery, then trim away the excess nylon organdy, using the embroidery scissors. Trim close to the stitching. It will not be necessary to trim and then go over the edges again as we did in the satin appliqué in Chapter 4.

If you wish to put sheer appliqué on a tablecloth or a garment that requires ironing, cotton organdy is the best. It is light and transparent, and will withstand repeated launderings without losing its crispness. And it has such a durable finish that it can be ironed.

Draw the motif onto the cotton organdy, and if you intend to do the corners of a tablecloth or other large article, do all the embroidery on the sheer material first except for the outer edges. This allows you to work without having the bulk of the article in the way. Sheer appliqué looks especially beautiful on each corner of a square or rectangular tablecloth. On a round tablecloth, the center is the place to do this kind of appliquéing.

After finishing the embroidery on the sheer material, pin it to the tablecloth and attach it by using a satin stitch. Trim away the excess sheer, then *turn the tablecloth over and cut away the tablecloth material under the sheer*. This leaves only the sheer.

If the material used in the tablecloth has a tendency to fray, the satin stitch serves pretty well as an overcasting stitch and

Fig. 5.5   Sheer appliqué on a tablecloth.

will prevent much of the fraying; however, there are several products on the market that will also help. Buy a bottle of "Fray Check" which comes in liquid form, and apply it to the raw edges. It will prevent fraying even though the article is washed numerous times.

For shadow appliquéing, use the same sheer material for both the garment and the sheer appliqué. The colors can be the same or contrasting. Let's use nylon organdy. Trace the motif onto the piece of nylon organdy, then pin it *under* the garment. With this material the pattern can be seen easily. Do all the embroidery

Fig. 5.6   Shadow appliqué.

on the good side of the garment, then turn the garment over and trim away the excess material from around the appliqué. Do not cut away the garment material as was done in sheer appliqué.

In both sheer and shadow appliqué you may find that it is much faster and easier to use the automatic rather than the free-motion setup.

CUTWORK

Cutwork is truly a beautiful form of "fancy" embroidery, but knowing what you do by now, it will be easy for you to execute. Although this type of work looks fragile and delicate, it is much more durable than it appears. This type of embroidery is done by using the buttonhole stitch, then cutting away the rest of

89

the fabric. Other stitches can be added to further enhance the individual style of cutwork. Connecting bars can also be added. Although cutwork is often found in collars, cuffs, and other garments, it is more often associated with both formal and informal table dressing. In formal table dressing it is usually better to use white on white; for informal luncheon sets, tone on tone.

BEFORE YOU BEGIN

Before beginning cutwork, it is always a good idea to completely finish the hems. This makes it much easier to center the cutwork design. There is a wide variety of hems, some of which you have already learned, such as the *shell stitch* and the *cord stitch*. We will describe a few other types of hems here.

Baby Scallops

One of the most popular hems in cutwork is done by using the automatic cam for *baby scallops*. This is done by setting the needle about ¼″ from the edge of the work to be done, applying the automatic cam design, then cutting away the edges left over. If you find the baby scallops too dainty, you can always go to the larger scallops such as you learned in Chapter 1.

If you make cutwork placemats, the matching napkins should always be square and large. Allowing for hems, it is best to cut them 19″ square. This will be more suitable for the more formal napkin-folding such as is seen in fine restaurants. You can make the edging on the napkins match the work on the placemats, and the rest of the napkin can be left plain or embroidered. (See page 96 for further hints on napkin-folding as it relates to embroidery.)

Crocheted Edgings

For those of you who like to crochet a nice edging, your marvelous zigzag machine can even help you there. Press under the edges, and set the machine on regular with a long stitch. Use a *wing* needle (also known as a #100) and *no* thread. Do a straight stitch along where you will be attaching the crocheted edging to make holes for the crochet work. If the holes are not visible enough, place a piece of dressmaker's carbon *under* the article, coated side up. The residue from the carbon paper will leave its mark, making the holes made by the wing needle stand out. You can then easily crochet the edging.

Fig. 5.7 Antique car—crochet-edged pillowcase.

If you don't crochet, you can buy some yards of Cluny lace and attach it by using a tiny zigzag stitch. Cluny lace closely resembles the handmade crochet or tatting, and comes in several widths.

Fig. 5.8 Dresser scarf showing Cluny lace.

Some machines have a hemstitch cam and all you have to do is use the embroidery foot or pattern foot, set the selector at "A," use Cam #140, with stitch width at #4 and stitch length at "A"+. Your needle size should be 100 to 120 and fine #70 darning thread is a must.

Fig. 5.9   Hemstitching on corner of napkin.

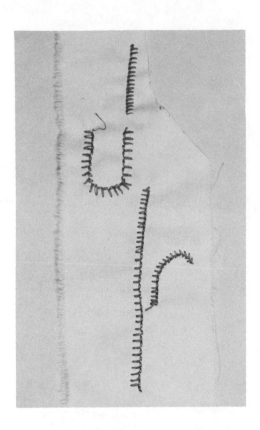

Fig. 5.10   Buttonhole stitch, blanket stitch, and hemstitch done by a cam.

Other machines sometimes have a cam that can be used for a blanket stitch, buttonhole stitch, or hemstitching. The stitching done by such a cam is shown in Figure 5.10. To use this particular cam in hemstitching, it will be necessary to cut the article you are making—say, a placemat—where you want the hemstitching to be. Then fold under both raw edges, and tape the edges to tissue paper no wider than your widest bight. Use a #100 needle and fine #70 darning thread for this. Tear the tissue paper away, and then do the outer edges, for in this case, there would be no point in doing the outer edges first.

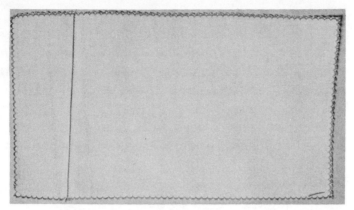

Fig. 5.11 Placemat with contrasting hemstitch.

No-Bar Cutwork (Broderie Anglaise)

On a scrap piece of butcher linen, trace the motif in Figure 5.12. Study the cam shown in Figure 5.10 and see if you have one like it. Some cams show the looped end on the left side as in the picture; others have the looped end on the right side. You can use either one just as long as you always turn your motif so that the looped side is next to the place where you will be cutting out around the motif. Where an "X" shows in a cut-work pattern, that is the area to be cut out *after* the buttonhole stitching is done. By adjusting the length and width of this cam, you can go from a blanket stitch to a buttonhole stitch, besides using it for the hemstitching shown in Figure 5.11.

Fig. 5.12 Cutwork motif.

ALTERNATIVES. If your machine does not have a buttonhole cam, try using the automatic buttonhole setup. By loosening the tension and using the hoops, you can get by very well. If you have no cams or automatic buttonhole stitch, you can still do cutwork. With a stitch length of 1½ and the automatic setup, do a linear stitch around the motif. When you reach the starting point, add a #1½ bight and go around again. Using good sharp embroidery scissors, cut out the "X" parts and cordstitch over the cutout edges.

You should be pleased with your work of art, for you have just accomplished Broderie Anglaise or no-bar cutwork.

Fig. 5.13   No-bar cutwork napkin.

Broderie Anglaise with Bars

This type of cutwork is generally used more on motifs with large cutouts. Surround the motif as you did in the no-bar cutwork, then with either the embroidery scissors or a seam ripper, slash each area—but instead of cutting away the area, push it to the wrong side of the work and secure it by either pressing or bartacking here and there. Use the same pattern you see in Figure 5.12 for the sake of simplicity, and use more complicated patterns after you become used to doing cutwork on the machine.

Refer to Chapter 3, where we learned the *stroke* stitch. We put the work into the hoops and change the setup to free-motion, if you remember. We must now do the stroke stitch from one buttonholed edge to another; this is much like making a bridge between islands. Stroke back and forth about four times, holding the two connecting islands very taut. Where you end, add a narrow bight and cover the stroke stitches with satin stitch;

lockstitch, clip, and go on. Plan your "maze" ahead of time in order to keep your "endings" to a minimum.

Look again at Figure 5.12. The "maze" that would be easiest involves starting at the end of the leaf and doing stroke stitches lengthwise to the other end. Then go back again and again; and then cover the lengthwise strokes with the satin stitch, returning to the point of beginning. Without clipping, do the satin stitch up the lengthwise vein until you come to the first line on the right. Stroke and satin stitch the right line, ending in the center vein, and then go on to the left line, repeating until all the connecting bars are finished. Lockstitch. Using a preplanned route of travel, you should only have clipped twice. Usually the folded-under cutouts add body to the article, but any untidy parts should be cut away.

Fig. 5.14   Placemat with bars.

Fig. 5.15   Broderie Anglaise with bars.

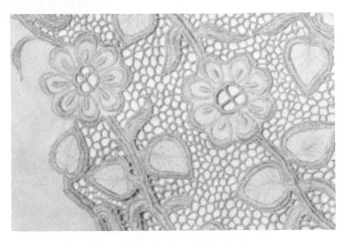

Fig. 5.16
Eyelet maker.

Eyelets

In conjunction with cutwork—or other kinds of machine embroidery, for that matter—you often will find that eyelets are a complimentary addition. In your accessories box you may have two or three sizes of eyelet attachments. Whereas in Chapter 1 we attached the flower stitcher and found it unnecessary if not impossible to use hoops, for eyelets the hoops are most helpful. So sprinkle your articles with eyelets here and there.

FOLDING NAPKINS. There is one thing you ought to remember when you embroider napkins, and that concerns their folding. There are many ways of folding napkins attractively, but the napkin that closely resembles a bishop's miter seems to be used more often and more effectively than many of the others. It is a good idea to fold the hemmed napkin in the kind of fold you like the best, then mark the place where the embroidery work would show most prominently when it is folded. Then do the embroidery work on the napkin.

Practice the folding technique shown in Figures 5.17 and 5.18 and soon you will do the folding without even thinking about it.

Fig. 5.17   Napkin-folding diagrams. Fold as in (a), then fold toward yourself along the dotted lines; it will then look like (b). Fold away from
yourself, then turn the napkin over; it will then look like (c). Pull out tips to
make dotted-line figures. Turn back tips A and B and tuck A into B. (d) Result.

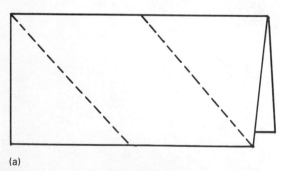

(a)

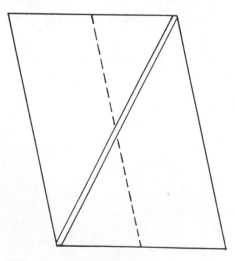

(b)

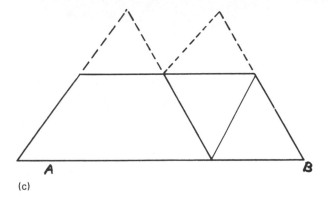

(c)

(d)

Fig. 5.18 Folded napkins. (a) Left, the papoose; right, the torch; (b) bishop's miter.

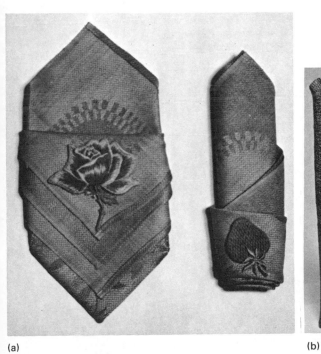

(a)

(b)

It is all well and good to decorate solid-colored articles, but sometimes we want to embroider patterned designs, too. In wearing apparel, for instance, polka dots, stripes, multifloral designs, and many others are so attractive that a wardrobe wouldn't be complete without them. If you enjoy the personalization of monograms but also like to wear patterned outfits, you can still have what you want.

Broderie Colbert

Take a piece of material left over from a polyester dress or shirt that is covered with a design. Use this scrap for the background of your practice piece. If your material is, for example, a red background with white polka dots, you can use either a plain white or a plain red piece of the same kind of material. Draw the motif desired onto the plain material.

Fig. 5.19 Broderie Colbert pattern.

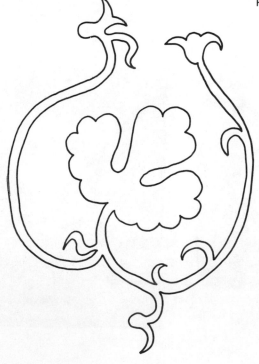

Now pin the plain material that contains the motif onto the polka dot material, and stitch over the motif with an attractive stitch. In this case a satin stitch made by turning the hoops as you go would accent the motif well. The thread must be in contrast to the plain material, so if you chose plain red, use white thread, or vice versa—both red and white being in the polka dot material. Cut away the excess material. This type of embroidery is similar to *Broderie Colbert,* which is used extensively in France.

Fig. 5.20   Polka dot dress with Broderie Colbert design.

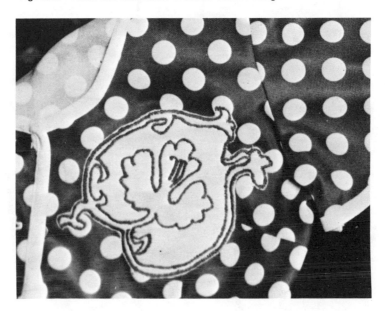

Chinese Calligraphy

We can all appreciate being happy, so let's try the happiness symbol shown in Figure 5.21. First, trace the pattern; then, with the automatic braiding technique (Chapter 4), follow the outline in braiding. If you want to put the Chinese Happiness Symbol onto a black background and use red braid, you may have to place the drawing on a window in order to reverse it. Then place the pattern onto the wrong side of the fabric and do a linear stitch around in order to make the pattern appear on the right side.

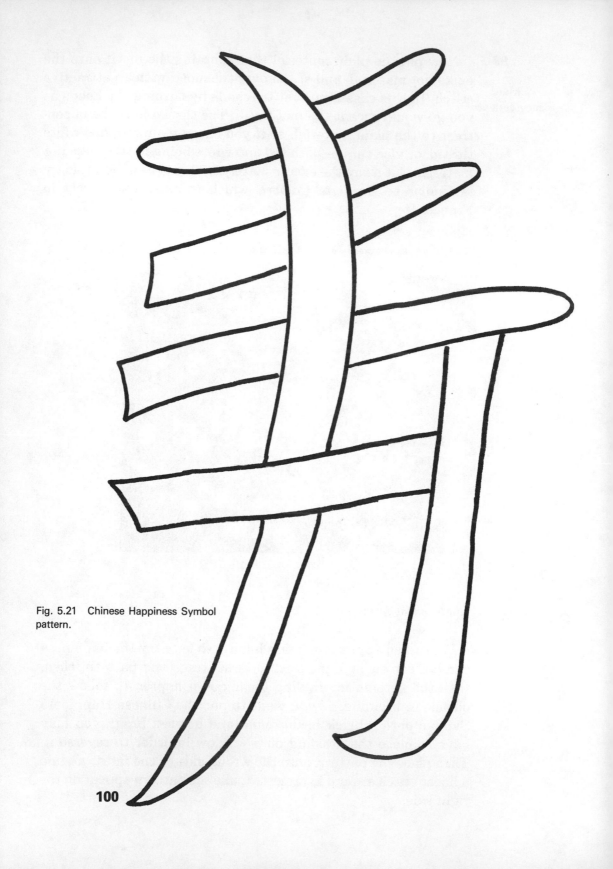

Fig. 5.21 Chinese Happiness Symbol pattern.

100

Beading

Once the symbol has been outlined by braiding, try adding some beads. Thread the beads on nylon thread in a color that will blend in with the background material. Thread the machine with either the transparent thread or a matching background thread, and set the machine up for bartacking. Bartack the end of the string with a bight of #1, but give the end bartacks a good twenty shots. This prevents the beads from rolling off. With your sewing machine screwdriver, push the beads along to where you want them, moving several, then bartacking with about ten shots, for here we want no buildup. Repeat and repeat until the whole string is finished. When you come to the end, make the higher bartack just as you did in the beginning. If you need to string more beads, repeat the whole procedure.

Fig. 5.22 Black blouse with symbol.

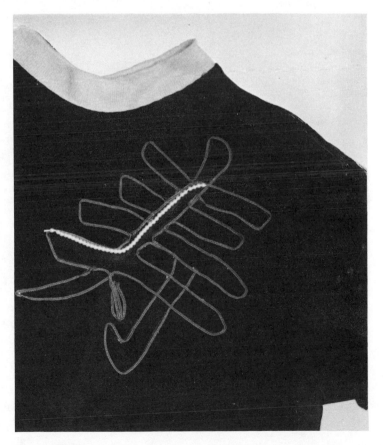

Sequins

Sequins can be done in the same way as the beads, or you can string them on a contrasting color of thread—something that will also blend well with the trim you are using. In Figure 5.23 the trim was purchased, but the plain silver trim did not show enough glitter, so the sequins were added, using the technique just mentioned. Transparent thread was used to bartack the sequins at the top and at the bottom.

We have pretty well covered sewing machine embroidery techniques by now. In the next chapter we will discuss the application of these techniques to various things you can make.

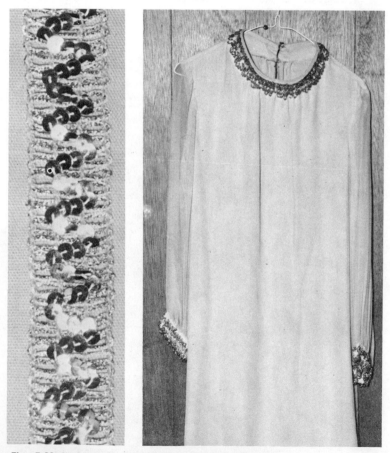

Fig. 5.23 (Left) Purchased braid with sequins added.

Fig. 5.24 (Right) Cocktail dress with beads added.

6 Other Things You Can Make

By now you can surely see that it is possible for you to decorate an unlimited number of articles with an almost unlimited number of stitches and combinations of stitches. All this using your sewing machine! So far we have looked at many "specials" —special threads, special materials, special effects. In this chapter we will talk about a number of specific things to make, and most of them will use stitches you have already become familiar with.

THE MEXICAN BLOUSE. Many people like Mexican blouses, and the one shown in Figure 6.1 can be worn by either sex. For the blouse pictured, automatic cams and free-motion stitching were used, and tapering, padded satin stitch, French knots, and flat embroidery were put to good use. Variegated thread was used for the stem work.

Fig. 6.1 Mexican blouse showing diamond smocking.

Smocking

Perhaps the most important part of the blouse is the addition of machine smocking, a beautiful type of machine fancywork. To do this, in cutting out the blouse, you must run the shoulder 2″ longer from the seam that goes into the collar and out to the seam that goes into the sleeve. All smocking is done before the garment is put together. Sew a row of basting stitches across the shoulder piece, using the same-color thread as the garment in the needle, but using a different color in the bobbin. Make another row alongside the first row, using the side of the presser foot as a guide. Repeat until enough rows are made; in the illustration there are nine.

Now pick up the top threads from both ends, and twist them together to keep them out of the way. Take the bobbin threads (they are a different color) and gather up the extra 2″. The shoulder piece should then be the correct size. Secure both ends of the basting threads so they won't pull out, by stitching across the thread ends.

104

Rickrack Smocking

There is a cam that produces a stitch resembling rickrack. It looks like the cam in Figure 6.2. If you run your rickrack stitch down those gathering lines as in Figure 6.2, you will make a nice-appearing machine smocking.

Diamond Smocking

If you would rather do your smocking just as it looks on the Mexican blouse, do the first row of rickrack stitch and when you reach the end of the row, pivot and come back up the next row. This results in *diamond smocking*. Do the sleeves the same way.

Fig. 6.2 Rickrack stitch and smocking.

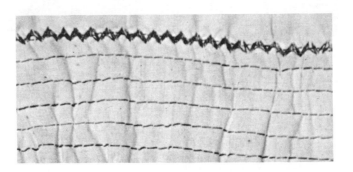

THE SLACK SUIT. The slack suit shown in Figure 6.3 is easy to embroider because you can buy iron-on transfers for crewel work. A simple paisley pattern was used on the hems of the suit. The pattern was traced onto a cardboard, then the garment material was marked with the cardboard for the pattern. If you decide to make this, you should trace the pattern on at least ¼" from the raw edges. In this case the motif was filled in with a tapering satin stitch, then cordstitched. The raw edges were then trimmed away with the embroidery scissors. Then, along the very edge of the garment, another cordstitch was applied. This sealed in any unsightly threads.

Here, one-half of a pattern is all it is necessary to use, because it is easy to turn the pattern over and reverse it. Some of **105** the flowers in the illustration were large enough in the centers

Fig. 6.3 Embroidered slack suit.

Fig. 6.4 Slack suit pattern and paisley pattern for around hemline.

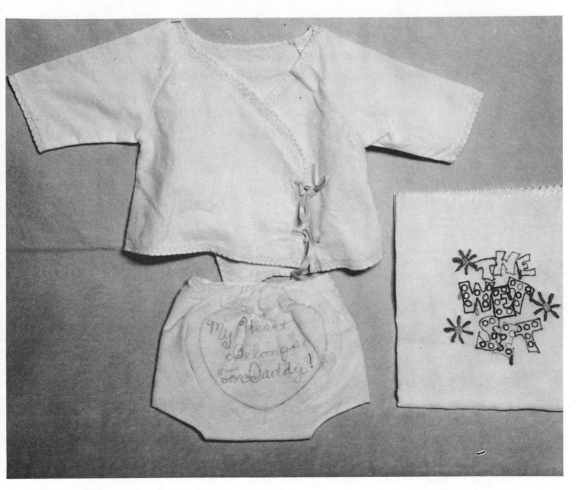

Fig. 6.5   Baby clothes.

that French knots would not have been the best choice, so eyelets were used instead. All the embroidery should be done first, before putting the garment together.

BABY CLOTHES. We must not forget the baby or the baby showers we are often invited to. A most welcome gift is diapers —and a dozen diapers with the top one done in fancywork quickly becomes a conversation piece at any shower.

TUFTED ARTICLES. Whether you need a headboard, a quilted wall picture, or a pillow, you may want to finish it up by tufting in some way. By far the easiest way is by button tufting. Make your own buttons with material that matches or contrasts with that used in the article. You could also buy buttons for this, but they must be shank buttons. (A shank button is the kind that has a metal loop which serves as a stem.) Put a paper clip through one button shank, open the other end of the paper clip, and stab it through the pillow or headboard to the other side. Push another shank button to meet the point of the paper clip; grasp that shank and squeeze the paper clip closed. The distance between the two sides of your pillow is determined by the length of the paper clip.

In stuffing a pillow, no matter what type stuffing you have used, as the stuffing relaxes around those shank buttons, a good pouf will appear.

Fig. 6.6   Button-tufted pillow.

COMFORTERS. There is no comforter like a machine-embroidered one, and it is easily made. All you have to do is to buy some washable satin or a satin sheet. Transfer your motifs and then embroider it. A plain cotton sheet could be used for the backing, or a complementary floral cotton sheet would work well. The cotton sheet would never be shown, because you would want to show the fancy top instead: however, it will prevent the satin comforter from slipping, so the cotton sheet is strictly utilitarian. The hems in this should be ripped out and pressed. If you own a zigzag machine, you should get used to making it work for you, and this is a good time for it. You can rip out the stitches in the cotton sheet hems with your "rapid ripper" attachment. Step on the pedal and rip away!

Fig. 6.7   Rapid ripper attachment.

RELIGIOUS VESTMENTS.   Such articles, especially the chasuble, are inexpensive to make if you make them reversible. Chasubles are the ornate full-length garments worn by clergymen over

Fig. 6.8   Chasuble.

other garments. They are made of different colors to commemorate special holy days. Because they resemble caftans, you can use a caftan pattern, a package of religious iron-on motifs, and moire taffeta for your material. Do the fancywork first; then, with the wrong sides together, stitch all around the caftan, leaving a very small place open (preferably at the neckline) in order to turn the material to the right side and press.

ULTRASUEDE ARTICLES.   Ultrasuede is one of the easiest fabrics to machine embroider. Gloves are inexpensive because they take very little yardage, so why not buy a pattern for gloves and get enough ultrasuede for one pair? After you cut them out, embroider a simple motif on them. From there you can go on to a vest and decorate that. Use cotton thread for decorative stitches; an ordinary needle works fine. If you want to use real leather, a cutting needle and long stitches are advised.

Fig. 6.9   Suede gloves.

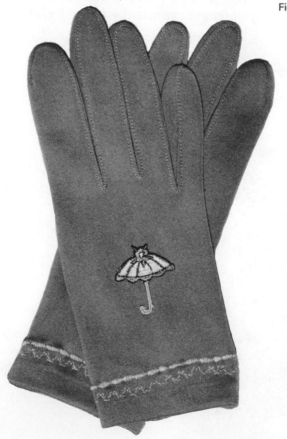

VINYL COVERS. Vinyl is used widely today and it is especially useful for shopping bags and book covers. It comes in plain-colored or patterned yardage, so it is just as easy to make vinyl book covers, for instance, and be able to protect the books from

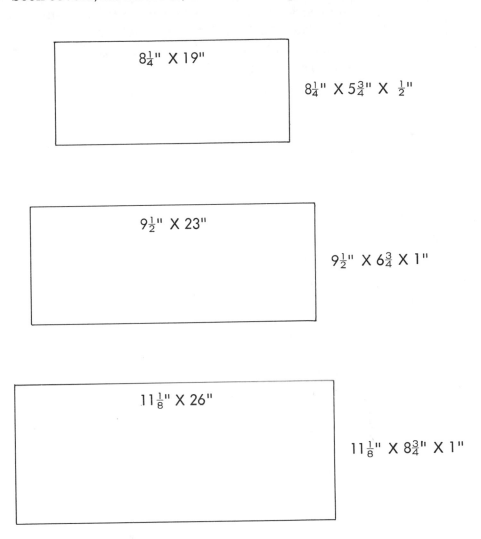

$8\frac{1}{4}$" X 19"

$8\frac{1}{4}$" X $5\frac{3}{4}$" X $\frac{1}{2}$"

$9\frac{1}{2}$" X 23"

$9\frac{1}{2}$" X $6\frac{3}{4}$ X 1"

$11\frac{1}{8}$" X 26"

$11\frac{1}{8}$" X $8\frac{3}{4}$" X 1"

Fig. 6.10   Book-cover dimensions.

rain, as it is to use any other material. The secret in working on vinyl is to press on a glide plate to the underside of the presser foot. Usually the roller presser foot is more suitable for vinyl, because this prevents slippage. The glide plate has a little protective paper on it; just peel it off and press the plate onto the presser foot. Sew with an ordinary needle; you can even sew through foam, plastic, or any plastic-coated fabric this way. Vinyl can be treated like ultrasuede as far as edges are concerned. There is no reason to fold over any edges.

If you have any difficulty on vinyl even after using these techniques, get a can of silicone spray and spray your machine bed. That should prevent any sticking.

Some book-cover dimensions are given in Figure 6.10 to help you in covering your books.

7 Take Care

Here we are, in the final pages of the book, and you now have literally hundreds of great things to make. Probably you have already completed some, and are basking in the glow of admiration from those who have seen the results. But by this time you also doubtless are aware of some of the "musts" involved in working with a variety of materials. Just to be on the safe side, let's review a few of the most important cautions, to insure that your creative machine stitchery is done with a minimum of frustration and a maximum of satisfaction.

PRESHRINKING

It goes without saying that we always want to preshrink by either washing or dry cleaning material before we begin to use it. Ultrasuede is about the only exception. Even nylon tricot should be preshrunk, if only just to relax it.

BLOCKING

For those of us who love to machine embroider, proper care of the finished articles is important, so we each should own a blocking board. This should be made from a piece of cellulose-type insulation board, for with this type it is easiest to pin and staple. Cover the board in the same way you cover your ironing board. (If you have an ironing board dressing, take a look at its padding, etc., and do your blocking board the same way.) Preshrink any fabric you use; then pull the cloth taut and tack it onto the back of your blocking board. Using a ruler and a laundry marking pen, make some 2" squares all over it. This serves as a guide for your blocking. The board can be put away and treated just like your ironing board.

To block dry, put the right side of the embroidery down on the blocking board and pin. Work along one side, following your 2" lines, and tack or pin along. Go to the other side, and pull the material smoothly, beginning at the center and moving outward.

Once the article is pinned securely, soak up a sponge and wet the entire article—both the background and embroidery work. After a day's time, the article can be removed.

Only block a wet article if it has become soiled. When this is the case, you must launder the piece by soaking it for a few minutes in cool water and soap, then giving it a gentle hand-wash for a minute. Rinse it in cool water that also contains a tablespoon of vinegar per half-gallon of water. This evacuates any residue from the wash water. Do not wring the article; rather, roll it up in a thirsty towel to get rid of the excess moisture.
114 Then take it to the blocking board and tack it right-side down.

Wool embroidery, like that in Chapter 4 and the embroidered wall plaque (Chapter 6) probably should be blocked, but embroidered clothing and large items are done equally as well if you place them on towels on the ironing board. The right side of the garment or article should be against the towel. Press lightly with a steam iron.

In taking care of placemats and napkins, launder them, and steam iron, then roll them on tubes with the embroidered side uppermost. Napkins—even though they may not have embroidery on them—should be rolled anyway, because they will be folded later.

An embroidered wall plaque, after hanging for some time, will tend to show some film. Put your vacuum on gentle suction by turning the nozzle piece that controls the suction, and gently vacuum it. Then spray on some "Stitch Clean." This will really lift the dirt right out of the stitches and then all you'll have to do is spray and wipe. In this way you never even have to remove it from the frame.

The 3-D wall plaques should be preshrunk first; then, once they are framed and on the wall, they can be taken down occasionally and gently vacuumed. If a plaque gets really dirty, use upholstery dry suds exactly as you clean the upholstery of chairs or couches.

Fake furs can usually be washed, but if you prefer, you can use "Fake Fur Cleaner," which is found at most craft stores.

Vinyl is, of course, washed with a cloth and soap much as you wash off the kitchen table, unless you prefer to use a vinyl cleaner.

Always use some sort of covering over your iron. This will prevent scorching. Use one even when you are applying iron-on transfers; often the transfer paper protects the place that is being decorated but the iron leaves a mark where the paper doesn't cover.

Ultrasuede is the most compatible material you will ever run into. You can toss it alone into the washer on gentle cycle—and toss it into the dryer too. However, when you have a large investment, such as three yards for a shirtdress and then several hours of machine embroidery besides, here is one time, even though it isn't really necessary, you can feel justified in sending it to the cleaner. Only petroleum solvent should be used.

Your metallic-threaded and beaded garments should also go to the cleaner. Of course if you wear your beaded garments very little, they won't have to be dry-cleaned often, and perhaps by then you'll desire a change in trim anyway. So take off the trim first and when the gown comes back from the cleaner, try out a new trim.

SECURING THREAD ENDS

Probably the most important thing to remind you about is to double-check all thread ends and make sure they are very secure. Use bartacks, backstitch, lockstitch, or "Fray-Check" a (commercial liquid), but do *be careful.* The superchain stitch, for example, cannot be locked in because you are using a single thread—no bobbin thread. It helps if you stop and cut thread ends as little as possible, but when you do stop, glue or bartack shortly after you have removed the superchain-stitch article. An adhesive interfacing can be used if added body is needed; otherwise bartack the ends or sprinkle with Texative fabric adhesive powder. This product comes complete with parchment paper. Sprinkle this powder along the thread ends, lay the parchment paper over it, and then iron it.

And so we come to the close of this book filled with information and illustrations to help you use your sewing machine creatively. However, we need not stop here, for creativity knows no limits. By now, you and your sewing machine are good friends, for you have shared many happy hours together. Live it up—sew it up —have *fun!*

Index